4386 Lindell Boulevard
St. Louis 8, Missouri

PRINTED IN U.S.A.

SERIES PREFACE

"Is it possible for an educational system to be conducted by a national state and yet the full social ends of the educative process not be restricted, constrained, and corrupted?" Thus did John Dewey in 1916 raise the problem of reconciling national loyalty with "superior devotion to the things which unite men in common ends, irrespective of national political boundaries." The problem itself is age-old—the ancients wrestled with it long before the emergence of the nation-state—but it has become ever more insistent with the development of modern national school systems on the one hand, and modern forms of warfare on the other.

Professor Scanlon's collection of hitherto inaccessible documents is designed to lend historical perspective to the continuing discussion of this problem. He views the educative process broadly, including mass communication and sustained cultural contact along with formal schooling. And he views it realistically, recognizing full well that political considerations are often dominant in the determination of school policy. His book ought to go far in advancing the cause of international education as an area for serious and systematic study in universities and teacher training institutions throughout the world.

LAWRENCE A. CREMIN

International Education

A DOCUMENTARY HISTORY

Edited, with an introduction and notes, by

DAVID G. SCANLON

CLASSICS IN

No. 5

EDUCATION

BUREAU OF PUBLICATIONS
TEACHERS COLLEGE, COLUMBIA UNIVERSITY
NEW YORK

Library of Congress Catalog Card
Number 60-14305

Printed in the United States of America
By the William Byrd Press, Inc.
Richmond, Va.

Contents

Part IV HELPING
PEOPLE HELP THEMSELVES

Part V COMMUNICATION

*International
Education*

A DOCUMENTARY HISTORY

International Education:
An Introduction

By DAVID G. SCANLON

"International education" is a term used to describe the various types of educational and cultural relations among nations. While originially it applied merely to formal education, the concept has now broadened to include governmental cultural relations programs, the promotion of mutual understanding among nations, educational assistance to underdeveloped regions, cross-cultural education, and international communications.[1] As a university discipline, international education is comparatively young, having made its entree in the decade after World War I as part of the optimistic effort of the twenties to develop a science of international relations. But the phenomena with which it is concerned are as old as nations themselves. This essay is concerned primarily with the phenomena of international education; but a secondary purpose will be to sketch the dimensions of one of the most rapidly growing fields of study in the American university today.

THE QUEST FOR INTERNATIONAL ORGANIZATION IN EDUCATION

The founding of UNESCO in 1945 represented the fulfillment of a dream that had fired the imagination of

[1] For an excellent introduction to the field see "International Frontiers in Education," ed. by William G. Carr. *The Annals of the American Academy of Political and Social Science*, Vol. 235 (Philadelphia, American Academy of Political and Social Science, 1944). A good brief account of the development of international education can be found in William G. Carr, *Only By Understanding*, Headline Series, No. 52 (New York, Foreign Policy Association, 1945). See also Isaac L. Kandel's classic, *Intellectual Cooperation: National and International* (New York, Bureau of Publications, Teachers College, Columbia University, 1944).

educators for hundreds of years. As early as the seventeenth century John Amos Comenius, the Moravian
churchman and teacher, proposed an international Pan-
sophic College dedicated to the advancement of mutual
understanding among peoples.[2] In succeeding centuries
Montaigne, Rousseau, Kant, and Fichte envisioned international educational cooperation as a step in the direction of world peace.[3] In 1754 the Swiss diplomat Emmerich de Vattel, in *Le Droit des Gens*,[4] urged the exchange of professors among various nations, arguing that
the peace and security of each nation was dependent
upon the peace and security of all.

But it was not until the peace congresses following the
Napoleonic wars that organized international efforts in
the field of education began to assume their modern
form. In retrospect these efforts appear meager, particularly when viewed against the great swell of nationalism
emanating from the French Revolution. For this was a
period in which patriotic sentiment was infusing every
aspect of culture. Each nation was looking romantically
toward that period in its history that represented its
"shining hour." In England, Tennyson revised and
popularized the legends of King Arthur. In France, Victor Hugo wrote of *Notre Dame de Paris*. Adam Mickie-
wicz, in his poetry, extolled the power of medieval Poland. Wagner used German folklore as a basis for many

[2] The universities of Ancient Greece, where students and faculty
from many lands gathered and exchanged information, provided
what many consider the earliest cross-cultural learnings. See John
W. Walden, *The Universities of Ancient Greece* (New York,
Charles Scribner's Sons, 1910). Likewise, during the Middle Ages
such informal exchanges occurred in the great centers of learning
in Europe, Asia, and even Africa (at Timbuktu). See Pearl Kibre,
The Nations in the Mediaeval Universities (Cambridge, Mediaeval
Academy of America, 1948); also Basil Davidson, *The Lost Cities
of Africa* (Boston, Little, Brown and Co., 1959).

[3] For the historical development of international organization, see
Inis L. Claude, Jr., *Swords Into Plowshares* (New York, Random
House, 1956) and L. Larry Leonard, *International Organization*
(New York, McGraw Hill, 1951).

[4] Emmerich de Vattel, *Le Droit des Gens,* 3 vols. (Washington,
Carnegie Institution of Washington, 1916).

of his works, and Verdi became identified as a composer of national Italian opera.

Bolstering efforts in the arts was the development of a new historiography. Treitschke[5] in Germany, Lamartine[6] in France, and Bancroft[7] in the United States began to write history as the genesis of national character. In Germany, Baron von Stein, the great liberal minister of education, sponsored a project to collect records and reports of the medieval period in his country; *Monumenta Germaniae Historica*[8] was the result. The English Parliament in 1800 appointed a special committee to publish the chronicles of medieval England; and in France a similar project was started in 1834.

The nineteenth century also marked the beginning of great national systems of mass education. The motives behind these systems varied, from the despotism of the Frederick Williams to the warm humanitarianism of a Pestalozzi;[9] but all were committed in one way or another to the advancement of national interests.

It is against this background of vigorous nationalism

5 See Heinrich von Treitschke, *Das Deutsche Ordensland Preussen* (Leipzig, Insel-Verlag, 193- ?); *Treitschke's Origin of Prussianism*, translated by Eden and Cedar Paul (London, G. Allen and Unwin Ltd., 1942); Adolph Hausrath, *Treitschke, His Doctrine of German Destiny and of International Relations* (New York, G. P. Putnam's Sons, 1914).

6 As a poet and historian, Alphonse Lamartine was a prolific writer. In his writings he showed a strange combination of medievalism, sentimentalism, monarchism, and Rousseauan naturalism. One of his best-known works reflecting his views is *The History of the Restoration of Monarchy in France*, 4 vols. (New York, Harper, 1851-53).

7 See, for example, George Bancroft, *History of the United States From the Discovery of the American Continent*, 10 vols. (Boston, Little, Brown and Co., 1854-74).

8 *Monumenta Germaniae Historica*, ed. by George Heinrich Pertz (Hanover, Impensis Bibliopolii, 1826) Vol. I. For an interesting account of Stein's work in assisting the *Historica* see J. R. Seeley, *Life and Times of Stein* (Boston, Roberts Brothers, 1879), Vol. II.

9 For more detailed studies of nationalism see Hans Kohn, *The Idea of Nationalism: A Study of Its Origin and Background* (New York, Macmillan, 1951). A standard reference on the relationship of education and nationalism is Edward H. Reisner, *Nationalism and Education Since 1789* (New York, Macmillan, 1923).

that the efforts of early pioneers in international education should be examined. For fundamentally all were out of step with the nineteenth century. In an era of nationalism, they spoke of internationalism. In an era of provincial loyalties, they argued for loyalty to mankind. And in an era of mass education for patriotism, they contended that the school was the only agency capable of advancing education across national boundaries. Little wonder that their proposals were viewed as radical, visionary, and utopian.

Pioneers of International Education

It was in the era of Metternich following the Napoleonic wars that the French educator Marc-Antoine Jullien published his first works on the need for an international commission on education. Jullien's proposals came at a time when the Holy Alliance had been formed and there was hope that the powerful nations might collaborate to end the problem of war. As the League of Nations became a vision of peace in 1919, and the United Nations in 1945, so did the Holy Alliance represent for many the end of armed conflict in nineteenth-century Europe.

Jullien's international commission was to be composed of educational associations from the various European states. The commission would gather statistics and other educational data from the member nations and disseminate them as widely as possible in an Educational Bulletin. Jullien envisioned not only a useful exchange of information but the growth of mutual trust and understanding among educators. If it was possible to bring educators together, then it might also be possible to bring nations together; and this was Jullien's ultimate goal.

When it became apparent that his proposal would not succeed, Jullien turned to international politics and organized a French Society for the Union of Nations. He failed here, too; but his notion of a Union of Nations became a forerunner of the League of Nations.[10]

10 Jullien's publications might easily have escaped notice altogether, had not Francis Kemeny popularized his pamphlet, "Es-

Sixty-eight years after the publication of Jullien's pamphlet, Herman Molkenboer, a Dutch lawyer who later became an educator, published another imaginative plan for an international education agency. The political climate of Europe, however, was quite different in 1885 from what it had been in Jullien's time. Well over a hundred noncommercial international organizations had been formed. The Paris Conference of 1856, while not successful, had introduced the concept of international arbitration. The first attempt to establish controls relative to the use of unusually cruel weapons had taken place at the St. Petersburg Conference of 1868. And Russia had been forced in 1878 to bring her peace treaty with Turkey before the European community for consideration and revision.

In the field of education, representatives from Germany, France, England, and the United States had organized a conference in London as early as 1851. John Eaton, United States Commissioner of Education, had presented to the International Conference on Education held at Philadelphia in 1876 a plan for a permanent organization that would be responsible for future international conferences.[11] Attending the Philadelphia meeting were representatives from thirteen countries and from nearly every state in the United States. Four years later, an International Conference on Primary Instruction held at Brussels had voted in favor of a world-wide council of education.

Herman Molkenboer deeply believed that governments would never disarm until people themselves were

---

quisse et vues préliminaires d'un ouvrage sur l'éducation comparée" (1817). An article by Jullien appeared in the *American Journal of Education* (Vol. I, July 1826) with the promise that others would follow; unfortunately none did. See also Marc-Antoine Jullien von Paris, *Skizzen und Vorarbeiten zu Einem Werk Über die Vergleichende Erziehung* (Berlin, Orbis-Verlag Ltd., 1954).

11 Department of the Interior, Bureau of Education, *The International Conference on Education Held at Philadelphia, July 17, in Connection with the International Exhibition of 1876* (Washington, D. C., U. S. Government Printing Office, 1877), pp. 84-89.

ready to work together peacefully. And people would not work together peacefully until they could be taught to do so. Emphasis, therefore, should be on helping teachers to develop concepts of world understanding. If all the children of Europe could be taught to respect their neighbors, world peace would be assured.

Molkenboer started a periodical entitled *Journal of Correspondence on the Foundation of a Permanent and International Council of Education*.[12] Published in French, English, and German, it was initially intended to serve as a means of disseminating educational information. Its purposes soon broadened, however, and it also became a vehicle for promoting the idea of an international council of education and world peace.

In retrospect, Molkenboer's proposals appear quite progressive, for he was really suggesting a political community of Europe. In the United States, he reasoned, people of various backgrounds had learned to live together peacefully. Despite differences in language, religion, and social background, it had been possible to create a federal government. If this were possible in the United States, why not in Europe?

Molkenboer presented his proposals for an International Council of Education in a pamphlet, *Die Internationale Erziehungs-Arbeit, Einsetzung des Bleibenden Internationalen Erziehungs-Rates*.[13] The Council would be both governmental and nongovernmental; members would represent national citizens' committees and ministries of education as well. Periodic reports would be issued on various educational topics and all members could call upon the Council for help in solving educational problems.

To stimulate interest in his proposal, Molkenboer formed a Temporary Committee for the Foundation of a Permanent and International Council of Education. By

12 Like Jullien's journal, Molkenboer's is referred to in secondary sources, but I have been unable to secure original copies.

13 Herman Molkenboer, *Die Internationale Erziehungs-Arbeit, Einsetzung des Bleibenden Internationalen Erziehungs-Rates* (Flensburg, Aug. Westphalen, 1891).

1890 several hundred subscribers had joined. Unfortunately, while Molkenboer received encouragement from the nongovernmental agencies, he received little assurance from governments. Within a short period the movement collapsed. Molkenboer left meager records— a few copies of the *Journal* and his pamphlet, *Die Internationale Erziehungs-Arbeit.*

The period from the close of the nineteenth century to the beginning of World War I witnessed the greatest effort in the history of civilization to build a realistic basis for world peace. The Hague Conferences of 1899 and 1907 [14] appeared to mark a new beginning in international arbitration. World-wide attention to the cause of peace was strengthened by the establishment of the Nobel Institute in 1904.[15] A Central American Court of Justice was created in 1908; and the Carnegie Endowment for International Peace was founded in 1910 with services devoted to "hastening the abolition of international war." [16]

Indeed, there was such a multiplicity of peace organizations that the need arose for some agency to coordinate their diverse activities. For this purpose the International Peace Bureau was created. The Bureau was, for the most part, concerned with providing materials and bibliographies on peace, arranging for international congresses, and making known instances in which nations had used arbitration as a means of settling disputes.

The world of education reflected this new development in many ways. In Great Britain the School Peace League was organized. Its aims were to promote, through the schools, international peace, arbitration, and friend-

---

14 See Antoine Pillet, *Les Conventions de la Haye du 29 Juillet 1889 et du 18 Octobre 1907* (Paris, A. Pedone, 1918).

15 Ragnvald Moe, *Le Prix Nobel de la Paix et l'Institut Nobel Norvégien* (Oslo, H. Ashehoug, 1932).

16 For the early activities of the Carnegie Endowment, see *Carnegie Endowment for International Peace; Summary of Organization and Work, 1911-41,* compiled by George A. Finch, Secretary, and others (Washington, D. C., The Endowment, 1941). See also Howard James Savage, *Fruit of an Impulse; Forty-five Years of the Carnegie Foundation, 1905-50* (New York, Harcourt Brace, 1953).

ship; to study, in meetings and conferences, the problems of racial relationships and the best means of eliminating prejudice; to study the history of the international peace movement; to promote, through lessons in civics, the development of a rational and humane national life and patriotism, and a sense of the corresponding duties to humanity; to print and circulate literature bearing upon these points among teachers of all kinds; to foster courage and devotion in the pacific spheres of industry and social service; and to work in connection with similar organizations abroad for the establishment of an international organization.

American educators who had participated in the National Peace Congress in 1907 formed the American School Peace League the following year. The League had as its objective "to promote, through the schools and the educational public of America, the interests of international justice and fraternity." [17] A council of fifty persons, with all states represented, governed the League. State organizations were formed, as well as one hundred local organizations. State branches provided materials to libraries, furnished speakers for Peace Day programs and helped high schools and normal schools organize student branches. The American League joined with similar groups in England, France, and the Netherlands in celebrating Peace Day or Hague Day on May 18 of each year.

In 1912 the National Education Association passed the following resolution praising the activities of the League: "The very material advance made in the cause of world peace during the past year encourages the National Education Association to urge a more widespread dissemination of knowledge upon this vital subject. We commend the American School Peace League as a channel through which teachers may procure such knowledge, together with suggestions for its presentation. The League has done excellent work in collecting and organizing

17 *American School Citizenship League: An Eleven Year Survey of the Activities of the American School Peace League from 1908-19* (Boston, American School Citizenship League, 1919).

material which appeals both to children and to adults; the accuracy of its statements is not questioned; its arguments are sound. The proposal to establish a world tribunal to fill the place of an international court for civilized nations is worthy of commendation and should have the earnest support of all teachers." [18]

The United States Bureau of Education published a special pamphlet, *Peace Day,* which offered suggestions for the celebration of the anniversary of the first Peace Conference at the Hague on May 18. William Howard Taft, in an article included in the pamphlet, wrote: "If the United States has a mission, besides developing the principles of the brotherhood of man into a living, palpable force, it seems to me that it is to blaze the way to universal arbitration among the nations, and to bring them into more complete amity than ever before existed." [19] Teachers in the United States requested fifty thousand copies of the little publication.

Although Jullien and Molkenboer had presented plans for an international bureau of education, Edward Peeters was the first actually to create a world center for educational information. In 1908 Peeters founded in Ostend a publishing firm, La Nouvelle Bibliothèque Pédagogique. Educators throughout the world saw the possibilities of the firm's serving as a center for the exchange of educational information, and urged Peeters to expand his quarterly bibliography on recent educational books, *Bulletin Bibliographique de la N.B.P.* The *Bulletin* was converted in 1909 to a monthly with the title *Minerva: A Review of Information Relating to Education and the Teaching Profession.* Peeters saw the publication of *Minerva* as the beginning of the International Bureau of Education. [20]

It is difficult today to appraise the effectiveness of

18 Fannie Fern Andrews, ed., *Peace Day,* Bulletin No. 8 (Washington, D. C., United States Bureau of Education, 1912), p. 11.

19 *Ibid,* p. 10.

20 For a description of *Minerva,* see Edward Peeters, *Comment L'Éducateur Peut-il Se Documenter?* Actes et Documents, No. 1 (Bruges, Bureau International de Documentation Educative, no date given).

Peeters' work in these years. Unfortunately, Ostend was in the war zone, and many of the records and documents relating to Peeters' work were destroyed. There appeared to be enough interest to encourage Peeters to write a constitution for his proposed International Bureau; but he unfortunately chose the Hague for his first conference (1912) at the same time that the second International Conference on Moral Education was being held in that city. Peeters had timed his meeting on the assumption that many who attended the Moral Education Conference would support his plan for an International Bureau. Unfortunately, only six attended his meeting. Nonetheless, the six revised the proposed constitution and set up a number of subcommittees to work on plans for expanding the Bureau.

From its beginning the Bureau faced serious financial problems. However, it continued to enlarge its work, issuing monographs on education in Japan, Panama, Colombia, the Belgian Congo, the Netherlands, and Bulgaria, and publishing a monthly periodical concerned mainly with correspondence by educators.

The sharpening threat of World War I and the problem of financial support ended the activities of the Bureau, which had remained a private institution. There were offers of governmental support, but too few and too late. The only other way of saving the Bureau would have been through greater support by educational associations around the world. Unfortunately, a great deal of moral support was accompanied by too little financial assistance.

A contemporary of Peeters who also contributed much to the cause of international understanding was the Hungarian educator, Francis Kemeny. Kemeny, impressed with the phenomenon of cultural borrowing, was convinced that all cultures were in part international, and that nationalism and internationalism could therefore be complementary forces. He expounded his ideas in a bulletin published in Budapest in 1901,[21] emphasizing

21 See Francis Kemeny, *Entwurf einer Internationalen Gesammt-Academie: Weltacademie* (Budapest, R. Lampel, 1901).

the need for an international bureau to undertake a program of international education.

International education, according to Kemeny, could be advanced in at least six ways: first, the publication of purely descriptive reports on education in various countries; second, the organization of international conferences for teachers; third (and Kemeny considered this basic to all others), the development of international agreements on the organization and structure of education; fourth, the formulation of international statements on the rights of man; fifth, the revision of textbooks to eliminate hatred and emphasize mutual trust; and, finally, a concerted effort to eradicate racial prejudice among all peoples. While Jullien and Molkenboer had dealt with cultural and ethnic problems, it remained for Kemeny to foresee the effect that race relations would have on governments and world politics.

Kemeny realized the necessity of both governmental and nongovernmental support for his proposed bureau. Without governmental support the bureau would be ineffective; without nongovernmental support it could fail to reach powerful professional and intellectual groups. Membership, therefore, would be composed of government representatives, professional organizations, and individuals interested in international education. Like Molkenboer, Kemeny anticipated the importance of a journal, and proposed that a periodical concerned with international education be published in French, German, and English, the cost to be borne by the governments that submitted articles.

It is a paradox that the best organized international education conference in history was called on the eve of one of history's most devastating wars. The work of planning the conference was largely that of the American educator, Fannie Fern Andrews. Miss Andrews had been responsible for the *Peace Day* pamphlets published by the United States Office of Education, and had been a leader in the American School Peace League. The success of *Peace Day* had led her to correspond with a number of teacher associations and interested groups in Europe. At the Eighteenth Peace Conference in Stockholm, she had been invited to present her plans for an international council on education. Following the lecture, she had traveled throughout Europe to enlist the support of teacher groups for her proposal.

The trip proved an education for Miss Andrews in the organization of European education, for it soon became apparent that for the School Peace League to succeed, it would require the support of Ministries of Education. Her original conception of an international council composed of nongovernmental associations was altered by her own experience and the advice of European educators who convinced her that any change in the curriculum of many school systems would depend on the willingness of the governments to cooperate. Originally she had thought of a council merely to put into effect the recommendations of the School Peace League. Her travels and experience led her to suggest a bureau that would include a permanent committee on educational research to serve as a clearing house for education; an international library; a translation division; and a publication division to issue an educational journal. She hoped that eventually the bureau would be as influential in education as the Hague Tribunal had come to be regarded in international disputes.

Miss Andrews returned to the United States with the unofficial promise of support from many educational leaders. With the approval of President Taft, she was named in 1911 as Special Collaborator in the United States Office of Education. The Hague stood as a symbol for all who were working in the area of international understanding, and for this reason Miss Andrews suggested that the first international education conference be called at that city. When approached by the United States State Department, the Netherlands government initially rejected the proposal, but later agreed, with the conditions that the conference be postponed until the following year and that an appreciable number of governments participate.

By 1912 Miss Andrews was able to report that a majority of the European countries were interested and would send representatives. Official invitations were issued by the Netherlands government to Belgium, Luxembourg, Denmark, Norway, Sweden, Germany, the United States, France, Greece, Great Britain, Italy, Austria-Hungary, Spain, Portugal, Roumania, Russia, Switzerland, and Japan. The agenda for the meeting ranged from the religious problem in education to training of the blind. Two months after the invitations had been sent, however, only France and Switzerland had accepted. The United States, which had taken the lead in organizing the conference, did not accept the invitation because of an Act of Congress (Deficiency Act, passed in 1914) which forbade participation in any international conferences without prior congressional permission. Miss Andrews waited months for Congress to accede; and the delay led to a postponement of the conference until 1914.

In January 1914 the Netherlands government again sent invitations. The interim period had not been completely without results, as it had given supporters of an international bureau the opportunity to draw up proposed articles for the establishment of by-laws. These articles were included in the invitations. American embassies throughout the world urged that all countries participate. Unfortunately, the response was discouraging; Europe was on the threshold of World War I, and felt little concern for educational conferences.

The war disrupted all communications in the field; but with its close and the opening of discussion on the proposed League of Nations, partisans of international education saw a new opportunity to create an educational agency as part of the League. Very early in the deliberations over the League Covenant, a group of women, with Fannie Fern Andrews among them, met with representatives of the Allied governments and presented a plan for an international office of education. Their proposal consisted of three fundamental arguments. First, they argued that the League's responsibility extended beyond simply preserving the peace. They thought of the League of Nations as an agency of civilization and contended that it could not escape the problem of education. For this reason, an international office of education was a necessity. Secondly, they argued that the success of the League would depend upon popular acceptance, and therefore it was important to teach young people about the League, its philosophy, and its organization. Finally, they emphasized that mankind would be liberated only if people had access to democratic education; hence the need for a massive League effort to advance the cause of universal schooling. The women proposed that an international office be established by a separate act in the League Covenant. Unfortunately, Paris was filled with committees with proposed articles for the Covenant, as Woodrow Wilson pointed out. Ultimately, the proposal came to naught.[22]

Committee on Intellectual Cooperation

During the period between 1919 and 1921 questions concerning education and international understanding were constantly before the League; and for this reason the League's Council considered a proposal by Léon Bourgeois that a committee of educators and scientists be appointed to study "international cooperation and educaion." The Council agreed upon a resolution that would have created a commission to study means by which an international bureau could assist intellectual cooperation and education. When the resolution was presented before the Committee on Humanitarian Questions of the League, a controversy ended any hope that such an international bureau would be created. The concept of "intellectual cooperation" was not challenged, but the word "education" proved controversial, since many nations, jealous of their sovereignty, feared possible infringement on their school systems. In the end, the

22 For an excellent summary of the activities of early pioneers in international education, see Pedro Rosselló, *Forerunners of the International Bureau of Education*, translated by Marie Butts (London, Evans Brothers, 1944). See also David G. Scanlon, "Pioneers of International Education, 1817-1914," *Teachers College Record*, Vol. 60, No. 4, January, 1959, pp. 209-19; and David G. Scanlon, "The Road to UNESCO," *Teachers College Record*, Vol. 60, No. 7, April, 1959, pp. 399-408.

League's Assembly did establish a Committee on Intellectual Cooperation; but the decision was made not to include education in the responsibilities of the Committee.[23]

The original Committee on Intellectual Cooperation of 1922 had as its president Henri Bergson, and included such scholars as Eve Curie, Gilbert Murray, Albert Einstein, and Jagadis Bose. The first proposal made by the Committee suggested an investigation of the conditions of intellectual workers in Central and Eastern Europe; studies of the possibility of expanding the international exchange of scientific publications; creation of an international fund for scientific research; establishment of a center for university information to encourage the exchange of professors and students; and the formulation of international copyright and scientific propriety right agreements.

The budget allotted for the Committee was only five thousand pounds, and even this was only approved after endless debate and controversy. The budget permitted only one meeting per year and an administrative staff of one assigned to the League Secretariat. By 1924, when it became apparent that the Assembly would not furnish adequate financial support, Henri Bergson appealed directly to the individual members of the League for funds. The French government agreed to support an Institute of Intellectual Cooperation in Paris with control in the hands of the League.[24] The Institute served as a clearing house and secretariat for a large number of

23 The Committee had strong support from such organizations as the Union of International Associations founded by Henri Lafontaine and Paul Otlet. The Union had as its purpose bringing together intellectuals and publishing the results of international conferences. Two hundred organizations had joined the Union. See Union of International Associations, *Sur l'organisation internationale du travail intellectuel à créer au sein de la Société de Nations* (Bruxelles, Union of International Associations, 1920).

24 For official reports of the International Institute, see League of Nations, *International Institute of Intellectual Cooperation*, Reports, 1925, 1926, 1927, 1929, 1932, 1934, 1938 (Geneva, League of Nations). In 1926, the Assembly of the League recognized the International Organization for Intellectual Cooperation as a technical body. The Organization consisted of the Committee, the Institute, and the various national committees on Intellectual Cooperation.

international organizations, among them the International Museum Office, University Information Center, and Educational Documentation Center.

In 1928 the Italian government offered to establish an International Cinematographic Institute under the control of the Committee. The Institute functioned until it was closed by Mussolini in 1937;[25] it encouraged the production, distribution, and exchange of educational films, and served as a center of information on educational film making.

Despite the handicaps under which it operated, the Committee did make a number of lasting contributions.[26] Its work in sponsoring international conferences later became a central function of UNESCO. Its mission to China in 1931 to aid in educational reconstruction helped establish the principle that it is a responsibility of international organizations to aid underdeveloped countries. Finally, numerous national organizations formed to support the work of the Committee set the pattern for later national UNESCO commissions.

The International Bureau of Education

Many of the early supporters of an international bureau of education viewed the establishment of the Committee on Intellectual Cooperation with disappointment. There was fear that the Committee's concern would be limited to strictly "intellectual" matters and not extend to pre-university education activities. There was no evidence that the Committee was willing or able to carry on the clearing-house function that many educators regarded as essential to any cooperative international en-

25 Examples of the early work of the Institute can be found in *Internationale Lehrfilmshau; Monatsschrift des Internationalen Institute für Lehrfilmwesen*, 1929-30 (Roma, International Institute, 1929-30).

26 See Henri Bonnet, "Intellectual Cooperation," in *Intellectual Cooperation in World Organization* (Washington, D. C., American Council on Public Affairs, 1942), p. 209. For the history of the International Institute of Intellectual Cooperation, see *L'Institut International de Coopération Intellectuelle, 1925-46* (Paris, Institut International de Coopération Intellectuelle, 1946).

deavor. Discouraged by the apathy of the League and yet determined to establish an organization that would serve the needs of primary and secondary education, an international group of educators founded the International Bureau of Education as a private organization in December, 1925, at Geneva.

For several years the Bureau attempted to carry on its work with contributions by individuals and corporate members. As usual, financial problems were pressing, and in an effort to expand its activities a new constitution was adopted in 1929 which made the Bureau an intergovernmental agency. Strong support came from the Swiss Government, but several of the larger nations tendered lukewarm cooperation at best. By 1938 there were only seventeen members, and unfortunately most of the governments represented were small powers. Although the United States has cooperated with the Bureau since the 1930's it did not join officially until 1958.[27]

The Bureau has made major contributions to education, largely through the leadership of such individuals as Pedro Rosselló and Marie Butts. It has published studies on comparative education, organization of education in various ministries of education, professional training of teachers, the use of school libraries, and the salaries of teachers in various countries. A central theme on problems of education has been selected each year for the Bureau's annual meeting. Since 1947 the annual conference has been sponsored jointly with UNESCO.

Conference of Allied Ministers of Education

While World War II temporarily ended international education cooperation, it did provide an opportunity for educational leaders to meet and plan future projects. In England governments in exile had been established by Belgium, Czechoslovakia, Greece, Holland, Luxem-

27 The Bureau started publication of a quarterly bulletin which includes information on education throughout the world and reviews educational works. In 1931 the Bureau requested annual reports from ministries. These reports have been incorporated in the Bureau's yearbook, which is now also published jointly with UNESCO.

bourg, Norway, Poland, Jugoslavia and France. The fact
that all these governments were (1) in close proximity because of the war effort, and (2) facing common problems
in educational reconstruction, led to a continual exchange of information and suggestions among the educators in exile. This informal exchange was formalized
in October, 1942, when Mr. R. A. Butler, English Minister of Education, called a meeting of Allied Ministers of
Education. In October, 1943, governments which had
sent observers were invited to become members. Official
delegates from the United States attended the meeting in
London in April, 1944, and indicated it was willing to
collaborate with other nations in establishing a United
Nations Organization for Educational and Cultural Reconstruction.[28]

At the first open meeting of the Conference on April
12, 1944, the United States delegation presented a resolution calling for a permanent organization. This proposal
was discussed and revised, and a tentative constitution
was sent to all members and associated nations of the
United Nations. Secretary of State Edward R. Stettinius
announced at the San Francisco Conference that there
was a proposal on the agenda for educational and cultural cooperation to be developed in the Economic and

28 See United Nations Information Organization, *Allied Plan for
Education; The Story of Allied Ministers of Education* (London, His
Majesty's Stationery Office, 1945). For a brief report of the Allied
Ministers Meeting, written by Ralph E. Turner and Hope Sewell
French, see U. S. State Department Publication No. 2221, 1944. Con-
cern for the role of education in the post-war world was expressed
by American educators throughout the war period. See the follow-
ing publications of the National Education Association and the
American Association of School Administrators, Educational Policies
Commission (Washington, D. C.): *Education and the People's
Peace* (1943); *Learning about Education and the Peace* (1944); *Let's
Talk about Education and the People's Peace* (1944). See also Erling
M. Hunt, editor, "Citizens for a New World," *National Council for
the Social Studies Yearbook* (Washington, D. C., National Council
for the Social Studies, 1944); Isaac L. Kandel, "Education and the
Post-War Settlement," in *The United Nations and the Organization
of Peace*, Third Report (New York, Commission to Study the Organization of Peace, 1943).

Social Council. Some members objected to the inclusion of the word "educational" and for a time there was fear that the same errors which had plagued the League of Nations would be repeated in the United Nations. Fortunately, agreements were reached; education was included in the final proposal. The San Francisco Conference formalized the place of the new agency within the United Nations. At the Conference for the Establishment of the United Nations Educational, Scientific and Cultural Organization, held in London in November, 1945, the Constitution of the new organization was drafted and signed,[29] and UNESCO was born.

UNESCO

The development of UNESCO since 1945 has been thoroughly covered by Walter Laves and Charles Thomson in *UNESCO: Purpose, Progress, Prospects*.[30] Suffice it here to say that for the past fifteen years UNESCO has developed programs in six major areas: education, the natural sciences, the social sciences, international cultural activities, mass communication, and technical assistance. In the natural science division emphasis has been placed on scientific research in the solution of social and economic problems, the dissemination through conferences and monographs of the latest discoveries in science, and the publishing of materials designed to improve the teaching of science in the schools. The social science division has concentrated on the publication of research monographs, the application of the social sciences to social problems, and the development of international understanding in the schools. The arts division has produced volumes on the art treasures of many countries and has also been concerned with the role of the museum as an educational agency.

As a result of UNESCO's success in applying academic

29 See David G. Scanlon, "The Road to UNESCO," *Teachers College Record*, Vol. 60, No. 7, April, 1959, pp. 399-408.

30 Walter Laves and Charles Thomson, *UNESCO: Purpose, Progress, Prospects* (Bloomington, Indiana University Press, 1957).

learning to the solution of human problems, demands on the organization have increased and the number of members has grown. Future UNESCO programs will undoubtedly depend upon what problems members view as most urgent. With the increase of newly independent countries in areas that are less developed technologically it is likely that additional attention will be devoted to efforts in social and economic development.

SOME CONTEMPORARY MOVEMENTS

In addition to the activities described above, three related movements since World War I have had broad implications for the field of international education: (1) textbook revision to eliminate hatred of countries and peoples; (2) governmental cultural relations programs; and (3) fundamental education programs.

Textbook revision until World War II was limited primarily to Western Europe, Latin America, Canada, and the United States. The rapid emergence of newly independent countries since World War II has lent greater urgency to the need for textbooks that will eliminate distrust and increase understanding of cultural variations.

The "cold war," the desire of new countries to have their societies known abroad, and the development of new techniques in the mass media have all contributed to the expansion of government cultural relations programs. At the same time, the science of propaganda has matured rapidly, making it increasingly difficult to differentiate between cultural and ideological efforts. Here is one of the most important frontiers in the field of international education.

Fundamental education represents the first international effort by technologically advanced nations to assist the less-developed societies through education. It is a revolutionary concept both in organization and content. Internal mass education and community development schemes have been carried on for decades by governments.[31] Fundamental education, however, as de-

---

[31] See David G. Scanlon, "Patterns of Fundamental Education," *Teachers College Record*, Vol. 58, No. 4, January, 1957, pp. 213-27.

veloped by UNESCO, is the first attempt to have international teams apply the findings of the social and behavioral sciences to education and cultural change.

Textbook Revision

In 1919, at the Congress of French elementary school teachers at Tours, Anatole France is said to have urged the teachers to "Burn the books which teach hatred, burn them all." In the reaction against the war, French teachers needed little encouragement to follow this advice.

Concern with textbooks can be traced back to the religious pacifists of the Reformation period, who urged that study of war be eliminated from all books. Little was done on an international scale until 1889 when the first Universal Peace Conference passed a resolution urging that the glorification of war be eliminated from textbooks.[32] By the close of World War I, it had become apparent to many educators that textbooks had played a role in the propaganda for war and they were determined to revise the content of teaching materials.[33] The National Union of Public School Teachers of France and the Colonies and the German Association of Radical School Reformers both demanded the elimination of hatred from school texts. To assist textbook writers, the German School Reform group actually prepared a series of synoptical history tables for the period 1500-1920.[34]

The movement appeared to be world-wide, for in 1920 the Japanese Association of Teachers suggested that the League of Nations establish a body to examine and criticize textbooks. In the United States, the Carnegie Endowment for International Peace sponsored a study of the problem of war in textbooks.[35] Similar studies were

[32] Albert Bushnell Hart, *School Books and International Prejudices* (New York, American Association for International Conciliation, 1911).

[33] V. H. Friedel, *The German School as a War Nursery* (New York, Macmillan Co. 1918).

[34] See UNESCO, *Looking at the World Through Text-Books* (Paris, UNESCO, 1946), p. 3.

[35] Carnegie Endowment for International Peace, *Enquête sur les Livres Scolaires d'Après Guerre* (Paris, European Center of Carnegie Endowment, 1923 and 1927).

sponsored by the American Association for Peace Education (1923), the National Council for the Prevention of War (1923), and the American Association of University Women.[36]

Along with the attempts to eliminate the "teaching of war," there was a movement toward education aimed at expanding knowledge and understanding of other cultures. A study by the Association of School Reformers in Germany, *Der Unterricht im Geiste der Völkerversöhnung* (1921), urged that the reconciliation of peoples be made one of the main concerns of teaching.[37] The Bureau of Cooperative Research at Indiana University, in addition to sponsoring a study of the attitudes of American educators toward peace, published a second volume concerned with teaching world understanding in public schools and teacher training colleges (1929).[38]

[36] American Association of University Women, *Report of the Committee on U. S. History Textbooks Used in the Schools of the United States* (Washington, American Association of University Women, 1929). Other publications of the University Women concerned with this area are *Literature and the International Mind* (Washington, D. C., American Association of University Women, 1933) and Esther Caukin Brunaur, *International Attitudes of Children* (Washington, D. C., American Association of University Women, 1932). See also Bessie L. Pierce, *Civic Attitudes in American School Textbooks* (Chicago, University of Chicago Press, c. 1930). Dr. Pierce's book was one of a series in "Studies in the Making of Citizens" edited by Charles E. Merriam. The series was published by the University of Chicago Press. Other books in the series related to this area include Herbert W. Schneider and Shepard B. Clough, *Making Fascists* (1929); Charles E. Merriam, *The Making of Citizens: A Comparative Study of Methods of Civil Training* (1931). Also see Carleton J. H. Hayes, *France, A Nation of Patriots* (New York, Columbia University Press, 1930). See also, Joseph Lauwerys, *History Textbooks and International Understanding* (Paris, UNESCO, 1953).

[37] UNESCO, *Looking at the World Through Text-Books, op. cit.,* p. 3.

[38] Henry Lester Smith, *Tentative Program for Teaching World Friendship and Understanding in Teacher Training Institutions and in Public Schools for Children Who Range From Six to Fourteen Years of Age* (Bloomington, Bureau of Cooperative Research, Indiana University, 1929) and Henry Lester Smith and Leo Martin Chamberlain, *An Analysis of the Attitudes of American Educators and Others Toward a Program of Education for World Friendship and Understanding* (Bloomington, Bureau of Cooperative Research, Indiana University, 1929).

Two years later, Jean Louis Claparède, the noted Swiss educator, published *L'Enseignement de l'Historie et l'Espirit International*,[39] which urged that history be taught in the spirit of internationalism. In 1932, Professor Rafael Altamira published *Problèmes Modernes d'Enseignement en vue de la Conciliation entre les Peuples et de la Paix Morale*.[40]

While teacher associations and private organizations carried on campaigns for textbook revision, the first formal international approval for textbook revision occurred in 1925 when the Casares resolution was approved by the Assembly of the League of Nations. As a result, the International Institute of Intellectual Cooperation prepared a study, *School Textbook Revision and International Understanding*, which was published in French in 1932, and in English in 1933.[41] The effects of the 1925 Resolution were limited, and because of the increased interest and demand of educational organizations, a second resolution stronger than the first, in that it placed greater responsibility on national committees, was passed in 1932.[42]

In 1935 the Institute of Intellectual Cooperation prepared a multilateral agreement for the teaching of history. Entitled "The Declaration on the Teaching of History," it was approved by the League Assembly in 1937, and fifteen nations agreed to accept its conditions. France, Great Britain, and the United States, however, declined to sign the agreement on the grounds that control of textbooks was in the hands of teachers and could not

---

[39] Jean Louis Claparède, *L'Enseignement de l'Historie et l'Esprit International* (Paris, Les Presses Universitaires, 1931).

[40] Rafael Altamira, *Problèmes Modernes d'Enseignement en Vue de . . . la Paix Morale* (Paris, les Presses Universitaires de France, 1932). For another study by Professor Altamira concerned with International Education see *Cuestiónes Internacionales y de Pacifismo* (Madrid, Bemejo, 1932).

[41] International Institute of Intellectual Cooperation, *School Textbook Revision and International Understanding* (Paris, International Institute of Intellectual Cooperation, 1933).

[42] For the text of the first Casares Resolution see League of Nations, *Committee on Intellectual Co-operation, Minutes of the Sixth Session* (Geneva, League of Nations, 1925), pp. 13-15. For the text of the second, see League of Nations, *Official Journal* (Geneva, League of Nations, 1932), Annex 1390, pp. 1782-83.

be enforced by any federal agency. Needless to say, the
lack of support from the great powers seriously hindered
the effort.

Some of the most productive work in textbook revision
has been carried on under various regional agreements.
Canada and the United States, France and Germany, the
Baltic States, Latin America and the Balkan States have
worked out viable arrangements for textbook writing.
The most successful work of this kind has been carried
on by the Norden Association in Denmark, Finland,
Sweden, and Iceland.[43]

*Governmental Cultural Relations Programs:
Communication and Propaganda*

France and Germany were the first to establish official
government programs in cultural relations, beginning
in the last half of the nineteenth century. The programs
differed in that the French effort was designed to promote French intellectual thought abroad, while the German was originally conceived as providing *Deutschtum*
(Germanism) for German nationals living in other countries. Of the two, the French effort is by far the better
known. France aided missionary efforts in Asia and the

43 For a history of the textbook revision movement until 1933,
see *School Textbook Revision and International Understanding*
(Paris, International Institute of Intellectual Co-operation, 1933).
See Albert Bushnell Hart, *School Books and International Preju-
dices* (New York, American Association for International Conciliation, 1910) for an early study of textbooks and international under-
standing. An excellent comparative analysis is found in "The
World War in French, German, English, and American Secondary
School Textbooks" by John Harbourt in the First Yearbook of the
National Council for the Social Studies (Philadelphia: McKinley
Publishing Co., 1931), pp. 54-117. Other studies which are con-
cerned with the treatment of foreign areas in American texts in-
clude Timothy T. Lew, *China In American School Text Books*
(Peking, Peking Express Press, 1923) and the *Treatment of Asia in
American Textbooks* by the Committee on Asiatic Studies, the
American Council on Education, and the American Council Insti-
tute of Pacific Relations (New York, American Council Institute of
Pacific Relations, 1946). For an account of recent work in this area
see *Laying the Foundation of "One World,"* by Professor Dr.
Jogindra Kumar Banerji (Brunswick, Germany, International Text-
Book Institute, 1957).

Middle East and, by helping to build schools and hospitals, furthered French culture in these areas. In Europe and the Western hemisphere France aided French schools and French institutes. An overseas cultural relations program was established in the French Ministry of Foreign Affairs with four divisions: universities and schools, art and libraries, travel and sport, and private cultural activities. Included in the latter were such agencies as the *Alliance Française,* which was created to encourage the study of French. On the eve of World War II, approximately 20 per cent of the budget of the Foreign Affairs Office was allocated for the cultural relations program.

In Great Britain private organizations had supported British cultural programs abroad for many decades. However, a more intensive effort was made in 1934 with the establishment of the British Council for Relations with Other Countries. The Prince of Wales, a patron of the Council, urged that the organization be concerned with the general interest of international understanding and not confine its task simply to fostering a nationalistic spirit.

The United States was the last of the major Western powers to create a cultural agency.[44] In 1938 the Interdepartmental Committee on Scientific and Cultural Cooperation with the Other American Republics and a Division of Cultural Relations were created. Again, as was true in Great Britain, nongovernmental agencies had been in some way concerned with international education since the birth of the United States as an independent nation. Officers from foreign countries had been trained at West Point since 1816. The Library of Congress in 1840 had started to exchange materials with foreign libraries. The Smithsonian Institute in 1849 had started an exchange service with similar institutes throughout the world. The first annual report of the

[44] See Ruth McMurry and Muna Lee, *The Cultural Approach* (Chapel Hill, University of North Carolina Press, 1947), and Harold Snyder, *When Peoples Speak to Peoples* (Washington, D. C., American Council on Education, 1953).

United States Commissioner of Education had contained information on education in other countries. John Eaton, United States Commissioner of Education, had recommended to the International Conference on Education, held at Philadelphia in 1876, a plan for a permanent organization that would be responsible for future international conferences. The Pan-American Union had been established in 1902. The United States Government had returned to China a large portion of the indemnity of the Boxer Rebellion for the education of Chinese nationals in the United States and for other educational purposes.[45] Funds that remained from the Belgian War Relief Commission were used to establish the Belgian–American Foundation under whose auspices exchange of students had been carried on.[46]

Private organizations and universities expanded their activities in the post-World War I period. The Institute of International Education was established in 1919, and four years later the International Institute of Teachers College, Columbia University, was founded with the aid of a grant from the General Education Board. The purposes of the Institute were: (1) to give special assistance and guidance to the increasing body of foreign students enrolled in the college;[47] (2) to conduct investigations

45 See Yam Tong Hoh, "The Boxer Indemnity Remissions and Education in China" (unpublished Ph.D. dissertation, Teachers College, Columbia University, 1933).

46 See, for example, Belgian American Educational Foundation, Inc., *Belgian and American C. R. B. Fellows, 1920-50* (New York, Belgian American Educational Foundation, 1950).

47 The increasing numbers of foreign students in the United States have led to studies evaluating their experience here and their roles when they return home. One of the best early studies is *The Foreign Student in America*, edited by W. Reginald Wheeler, Henry H. King, and Alexander B. Davidson (New York, Association Press, 1925). More recent studies include John Useem and Ruth Hill Useem, *The Western Educated Man in India* (New York, The Dryden Press, 1955); Ralph L. Beals and Norman D. Humphrey, *No Frontiers to Learning: The Mexican Student In The United States* (Minneapolis, University of Minnesota Press, 1957); Franklin D. Scott, *The American Experience of Swedish Students* (Minneapolis, University of Minnesota Press, 1956); Richard D. Lambert and Marvin Bressler, *Indian Students on an American Campus* (Minneapolis, University of Minnesota Press, 1956); John

into educational conditions, movements, and tendencies in foreign countries; and (3) to make the results of such investigations available to students of education throughout the world to promote the course of education. The Carnegie Foundation, the Doris Duke Foundation, the John Simon Guggenheim Foundation, the Rockefeller Foundation, and the W. K. Kellogg Foundation were among the private organizations that assisted the cause of international education.

Since the close of World War II the increasing participation of the United States in world affairs has led to an expansion of federal international programs. Today there is hardly a department of the United States government that is not involved in some form of international education.[48]

Recent years have also witnessed a growing awareness on the part of all governments that information programs are a necessity in the field of international relations. As a result, practically every government produces films, filmstrips, brochures, posters, and journals.[49] The objec-

---

W. Bennet, Herbert Passin, Robert K. McKnight, *In Search of Identity: The Japanese Overseas Scholar in America and Japan* (Minneapolis, University of Minnesota Press, 1958); Jeanne Watson and Ronald Lippit, *Learning Across Cultures: A Study of Germans Visiting America* (Ann Arbor, University of Michigan, 1955).

[48] See U. S. Congress House *Government Programs in International Education*, 85th Congress, 2d Session, H.R. No. 2712 (Washington, D. C., Government Printing Office, 1959) for a complete survey of official U. S. activities in international education. Since World War II American universities have increased their relationships with overseas institutions. See *The International Programs of American Universities: An Inventory and Analysis* (East Lansing, Institute on Overseas Programs, Michigan State University, 1958) for a general account of American universities engaged in overseas programs. See also the "Studies in Universities And World Affairs" prepared for the Carnegie Endowment for International Peace and published by the American Council on Education (Washington, D. C.). Particular mention should be made of *American College Life as Education in World Outlook,* by Howard E. Wilson, published in 1956, and *University Research on International Affairs,* by John Gange, published in 1958.

[49] For a study of the expansion of mass media see UNESCO, *World Communication: Press, Radio, Films, Television* (Paris, UNESCO, 1956).

tives of governments in this respect are quite similar: to
develop outside their own countries a sympathetic reception for their political, social, and cultural policies. Yet
the line between information and propaganda is rarely
clear; and with all the mass media at their disposal it is
relatively easy for governments to go beyond simple information to purvey skillful and carefully conceived
propaganda. Attempts have been made to limit propaganda by agreements among nations, but there have
been no notable successes to date.[50]

It may be possible to reach certain agreements relative
to the content of cultural publications under the supervision of international educational agencies, but there
is no evidence at the present time to suggest that such
agreements will actually preclude propaganda activities.
International groups like UNESCO are increasingly using the mass media to attack common international
problems and producing cultural materials that may help
counteract international propaganda. There is no doubt,
however, that the development of modern mass media has
literally transformed both the concept and the problem
of international education. Mass education, diplomacy,
and even war have already been deeply affected. And the
student of international education must be prepared to
look in quite different ways at some of the traditional
problems of cross-cultural understanding.

Fundamental Education

With the establishment of UNESCO, one of the first
problems the members had to face was the question of
priorities. The educational system of Europe had to be
reconstructed; those who had worked closely with the
Committee on Intellectual Cooperation were anxious to
revive cultural and intellectual exchanges; and the new
nations that had emerged in Asia were eager to have
educational assistance in building educational systems.
While professors might be sent to the underdeveloped
countries to help build and strengthen colleges and uni-

50 See L. John Martin, *International Propaganda* (Minneapolis,
University of Minnesota Press, 1958).

versities, the basic problem was how to introduce an education that would reach the people of the vast, underdeveloped rural regions of the world where the need for progress in education, health, and social and scientific development was pressing. Fundamental education was conceived as a cultural transformation leading to *self*-development under the leadership of foreign specialists or under educated nationals working in depressed areas within their own countries.[51]

Throughout the centuries private and governmental groups have sponsored various kinds of educational programs aimed at promoting literacy, health, and agriculture. The Catholic missionaries in Mexico who established community centers for Indians;[52] Protestant missionaries who served as specialists in health and agriculture; Buddhist and Islamic teachers who taught illiterates;[53] the demonstration techniques developed by Seaman A. Knapp and the Penn School of South Carolina—all are examples of early approaches to fundamental education.

The first modern mass education movement having as its goal literacy and self-improvement in areas of health and agriculture was started by James Yen of China. Yen

51 In the United States, concepts of fundamental education are described by Edmund de S. Brunner and E. Hsin Pao Yang in *Rural America and the Extension Service* (New York, Bureau of Publications, Teachers College, Columbia University, 1949). For other examples see Orie Hatcher, *A Mountain School* (Richmond, Garrett and Maisie, 1939; Archie Beverly, *The Development of the Whitmell Farm Life School* (New York, Vantage Press, 1955); Harnett Kane, *Miracle in the Mountains* (Garden City, Doubleday & Co., 1956); and Elsie R. Clapp, *Community Schools in Action* (New York, Viking Press, 1939). For descriptions of projects in other areas, see Lloyd H. Hughes, *The Mexican Cultural Mission Programme* (Paris, UNESCO, 1950) and David G. Scanlon, "Fundamental Education in Liberia, West Africa," *Teachers College Record*, Vol. 55, No. 2, November, 1953, pp. 70-77.

52 An excellent account of cultural change effected by the missions in California can be found in Zephyrin Englehardt, *The Missions and Missionaries of California*, 5 vols. (San Francisco, James Barry, 1915).

53 See J. S. Furnivall, *Educational Progress in Southeast Asia* (New York, Institute of Pacific Relations, 1943).

had served as educational secretary to the two hundred thousand Chinese who had been brought to France as laborers during World War I, and under his direction literacy classes were started. The success of his work in France led Yen to continue his method when he returned to China. Under his direction, a scientific selection was made of the thirteen hundred characters most frequently used in the spoken Chinese language; and these characters became the basis for the literacy instruction.

Although Yen's original interest had been in literacy, the movement soon came to embody elements of community development. Under the intensive experiment plan, a region would be selected, and work in the region would be continued until illiteracy was wiped out, health measures had been introduced, and agricultural reforms effected.

Several years after Yen began his efforts, Frank Laubach undertook a similar campaign in the Philippines, starting with literacy and, like Yen, enlarging to include the area of community development. Similarly, Mexico created "cultural missions" to develop popular interest in economics and social improvement. In Turkey, under Attaturk, the *halkevis* (folk house) was established to serve as a welfare center for a network of villages.[54]

Thus, although the expression "fundamental education" was coined by UNESCO in 1946, there had been many programs based on the concept in the past. Fundamental education is fundamental in the sense that it provides the basic education needed for improvement. Traditionally, it has been concerned with literacy, health, and agriculture, but it has also included such areas as the organization of cooperatives, road building, and the encouragement of indigenous industries.[55]

54 A good description of the *halkevis* can be found in Donald B. Webster, *The Turkey of Attaturk* (Philadelphia, American Academy of Political and Social Science, 1939).

55 National Society for the Study of Education, *Community Education: Principles and Practices from World-Wide Experience*. Fifty-eighth Yearbook, ed. by Nelson B. Henry (Chicago, University of Chicago Press, 1959).

CONCLUSION

UNESCO is far removed from the simple proposal of Marc-Antonine Jullien. International education has progressed as international organization has developed. As the forces of international politics have compelled nations to work more closely together to solve common problems there has been an increasing awareness of education as a major international concern.

It is for this reason that such concerted effort is being made by UNESCO, I.C.A., the Colombo Plan, and various regional organizations to use education as a means of raising the standards of living in less developed societies. The fact that thousands of people from many societies are meeting under varying circumstances has increased interest in what has come to be called "cross-cultural education." There is an awareness that international education will have to make greater use of the behavioral sciences to investigate in a more systematic way what takes place "when peoples meet." [56] There is also a recognized need for more study of the process of international organization. Administrative procedures involving varying concepts of organization can be a problem. It is for this reason there have been continuing appraisals, not only of programs of international education, but of the process under which such programs are developed.

There is every evidence that all areas of international education will expand vastly in the immediate future. There is scarcely an activity in the field that is not developing at a rapid pace. At this time therefore it is well to review the foundations upon which present programs have been built. For several generations attempts at international education have been suffused with a warm humanitarianism that has been idealistic at best, but on occasion sentimental and politically unrealistic. The

---

[56] The term "cross-cultural education" is being used to describe a number of varying situations. For the purpose of this essay I have used the term to describe the learning that occurs when people from one country come into contact with people from another.

problem for international educators today seems to be to join this commendable humanitarianism to programs of imaginative research in the social sciences that will yield intelligent and politically viable programs. Only through some workable union of sympathy and science can the study of international education be of genuine assistance to statesmen and school men throughout the world.

Part I PIONEERS OF INTERNATIONAL EDUCATION

→>X<←

A College of Light*

JOHN AMOS COMENIUS

As a theologian, Bishop of the Moravian Church, and educator, Comenius was shocked by the excesses of the political and religious wars that swept Europe in the early decades of the seventeenth century. He was later to win fame throughout Europe as an educator, his services sought by England, France, and Sweden. In the Panorthosia, *Comenius urges the establishment of a College of Light that would serve as an international office of education and a universal academy. In the selections from the* Panorthosia *that follow, Comenius discusses the College of Light in connection with the necessity of international cooperation.*

> *Of the necessity of making permanent all things which have once been properly constituted, through three supreme colleges or tribunals, the bonds of the happiness of the ages; and what they are to be like.*

Once things have been so reformed that all things—philosophy, religion and polity—are indeed universal, the learned men will be able to collect and try the truth and impress it on the minds of men; men of religion will be able to draw souls from the things of the world to those of God; and men of politics will be able to preserve peace and quiet everywhere; as it were challenging each other to holy emulation, that each in his own sphere should promote the well-being of the human race as best he can.

* *John Amos Comenius, 1592-1670: Selections,* Introduction by Jean Piaget (Paris, UNESCO, 1957), pp. 157-173.

2. The saying of Cicero is admirable: 'It is unworthy of the dignity of a wise man to believe what is false or to defend without hesitation anything accepted without due investigation.' Similarly let our theologians, who are to lead others to holiness, hold it incompatible with their honour to do or tolerate anything which is not holy; and our men of politics, the men of peace, hold it unworthy of their honour to give cause for dissension or to bear with it, not to speak of defending it.

3. In the meantime, however, since what is everybody's job is done by nobody, men outstanding among their fellows must be chosen to perform this special task; they will keep watch as from a high tower, not to allow anything unworthy of the reformed state of things (i.e., that nothing false, impious or troublesome should creep in).

4. If this is not done we cannot hope for anything firm and lasting; for the history of all ages tells us that even the best constituted things, if not preserved in good order, grow weak and loosen, in the end falling apart and slipping back into their old disorder.

5. Look at the Israelites, what ill counsel they followed, when after entering the Promised Land they gave themselves up to domestic employment, laying aside their arms and keeping no watch on the remnants of their enemies: the latter gathered their strength again, to the Israelites' distress. Warned by their example, and by thousands of others, let us learn to fish with care! When we have so organized human society that the learned teach their learning, the men of religion raise men to God, and the rulers govern, let us give them custodians to aid them. Then it will not be so easy for indifference or torpor or sleepiness to return, for the enemy to find an opportunity to return while men sleep, and sow his tares.

6. Let the learned, I say, be given vigilant men who will rouse them to action to drive out any ignorance or error still hiding in man's mind. Let them be given to the men of religion, that with their help all atheism, epicurism and profanity still to be found may be driven

out. Let the powerful be given custodians of their power, lest by abuse of emulation the seeds of discord should return; or if they return, that they should be weeded out in time and wisely, nor otherwise than to the private and the public weal of all.

7. Let us oppose the danger we fear (that universal matters concerning the order and well-being of the human race may become loose and fall apart) with a measure than which no more efficacious can be found: that perpetual custodians be appointed for the things once constituted piously; they will give their constant attention to see whether the schools are truly enlightening men's minds, whether the temples are truly moving men's hearts, and whether the body of governors truly protects the public peace; and will not allow aberrations either to creep in or to grow stronger again.

8. It is true that we shall have in every school, every church and every State custodians of law and order (I have in mind the proctors, presbyters and senators); but even so a constant gradation is necessary in all things, which should not be interrupted until it reaches the highest point in any particular sphere, and most of all where the eternal foundations of the common weal are to be strengthened. For just as people living together form a family, families together a community, communities together a province, provinces a State, and the whole community of States forms one commonwealth of the whole human race, so let each home have its tribunal, each community, each province, each State, and finally the whole world. Similarly the authorities placed over the schools and the churches to supervise their order and their progress must have their degrees, up to the highest point, where they are concentrated and where is to be found the power keeping all men and all things within the bounds of the common weal.

9. But there should be more than one such custodian of human well-being, as Christ, Wisdom Eternal, has taught us, in the famous words of St. Matthew's Gospel (xxiii. 8, 9, 10) forbidding men to set up the rule of one man, the leadership of one man, the wisdom of one man,

among themselves. He told them not to be called upon the earth

1. Rabbi			the learned
2. Father	Which it is fitting		ecclesiastics
3. Master	to use for		men of State.

That nothing should be instituted otherwise than that all men should live as brethren, all with one Father who is in heaven, and who gave us one Master and leader, Christ.

10. Therefore colleges will be set up in each of these three spheres, the highest authority in each of which will be that Hermes Trismegistos (God's greatest triple interpreter for man, supreme prophet, supreme priest, supreme king) Christ, who alone rules by His ability to dispose of all things with validity. In order to maintain order, then, some men everywhere will be placed above others, so that through all degrees of subordination Christ's school, Christ's temple and Christ's kingdom will be firmly held together everywhere.

11. Would it not therefore be wise to set up three tribunals to which all controversies which may perhaps arise among the learned, the men of religion and the rulers should be referred? To prevent by their vigilant care discord and schism among the first, second, or last of these? Otherwise we have no hope at all of bringing stability to what has been reformed.

12. It will be wise to distinguish them also by their names, the tribunal of the learned to be called the College of Light, the tribunal of the churchmen the Consistory, the political tribunal the Dicastery.

13. It will be the task of the College of Light to ensure it will nowhere among the peoples be necessary to teach anyone anything, much less that anyone should be ignorant of anything essential, but that all men should be taught by God. That is to say, to provide opportunity for the eyes of all men throughout the world to turn towards that light in which all may see the truth for themselves, and in which they will never again be able to admit errors or hallucinations.

14. It will be the task of the oecumenical Consistory to ensure that all the bells of the horses and all the pots, etc., should be 'Holiness unto the Lord' (Zechariah, xiv. 20) and that 'there shall be no more utter destruction, but Jerusalem shall be safely inhabited' (v. 11). That is to say, that the whole land and the fullness thereof should be dedicated to Christ; that there should be no scandal, no scandalous writings or carvings or pictures on any vases, etc., but rather let all things be full of holy emblems that every man, wherever he may turn, may find food for pious meditation.

15. Finally it will be the task of the Dicastery of Peace to see that no one nation rises against another, and that no man dare to stand up and teach men to fight or to make weapons, and that no swords or spears shall be left that have not been beaten into ploughshares and pruning hooks. (Isaiah, ii. 4.)

16. Therefore let all colleges of learned men (such as the present Accademia dei Lincei in Italy, the Collège des Roses in France, the Fruchttragender in Germany, etc.) combine to form one College of Light for the eternal Father of Light Himself calls them to unite in the community of light. For He said: 'Moreover the light of the moon shall be as the light of the sun, and the light of the sun shall be sevenfold, as the light of seven days, in the day that the Lord bindeth up the breach of his people, and healeth the stroke of their wound.' (Isaiah, xxx. 26.) 'And it shall come to pass, that at evening time it shall be light.' (Zechariah, xiv. 7.)

17. And let all the consistories or presbyteries of the Christian churches (such as those of the Greeks, the Romans, the Abyssinians, the Evangelicals, etc.) join in one universal church consistory, as is foreseen in the symbol of Jerusalem, 'builded as a city that is compact together, for there are set the thrones of judgement, the thrones of the house of David.' (Psalm 122. 3, 5.) Understand by this the Son of David, ruling His kingdom in such a way that there may be those who 'sit on thrones judging the twelve tribes of Israel' (Luke, xxii. 30), i.e., the whole church.

18. And let all the tribunals of the world become one tribunal of Christ, for when all the kingdoms of the world have been given Him (Psalm 72. 11, Daniel VII. 14, Apocalypse, XI. 15) 'a king shall reign in righteousness, and princes shall rule in judgement'. (Isaiah, XXXII. 1.)

19. Care must be taken to choose these select men from among the best, i.e., the wisest of the wise, the most pious of the men of religion, the most powerful of the powerful. Nor should the other desirable qualities be neglected, for wise men will be better guided by a wise man who is at the same time pious and powerful, than by one who is merely wise; the powerful by a powerful man who is also wise and pious, than by one who is powerful without either wisdom or piety.

20. Only then will the members of the College of Light in truth and in deed be what Seneca called philosophers: teachers of the human race; and the members of the universal consistory will in truth and in deed be what Christ called them: the light of the world and the salt of the earth; and the universal rulers will in truth and in deed be what David called them: the shields of the earth, or the defenders of God on earth. (Psalm 47. 9.)

21. Their highest virtue will be supreme concord and perpetual unanimity for the well-being of the human race; as if they were one heart, or one soul of the world, made up of intellect, will and executive faculties. Some philosophers have doubted up to now whether the world has a soul; they will cease to doubt when they see that these ministers of light, peace and zeal are as one mind and inspire one life and one salvation in the world.

22. They will work together in concord to bring into the world light, peace and happiness in the latter day; to raise the house of the Lord above the summits of the mountains (so that all the peoples cannot but see this light, and the peace and happiness which follow it); to tame the monsters, like Samson and Hercules, should any appear; to stand like cherubim with flaming swords at the gates of this Paradise (the reformed church) and drive away all impurities; and like Noah to gather into the ark of light, peace and salvation all living creatures to be saved from destruction.

23. If anyone should ask how many of these progenitors of our common happiness there should be, it would seem best for every kingdom or republic to have two, three, four or more custodians of the light for itself, as many custodians of the peace and no fewer custodians of piety. Let any of these colleges have one superior among them; and these again one superior in Europe, one in Asia, one in Africa, etc. All these together will be that Senate of the world, those teachers of the human race, that light of the world, those shields of the earth, who will see to it that philosophy is the home and bastion of truth throughout the world, that religion is the home and bastion of piety, and that polity is the home and bastion of peace and security throughout the world.

24. If I am asked about the place, and whether it is necessary that they live together there—I do not think so. Leaving their bodies where they will they can live together in the spirit, all doing the same things each in his own place, and giving news each year of gains for the kingdom of Christ, in light, peace and holiness. This applies particularly to scholars, who are most closely concerned with this commerce of minds and nations. Funds and means will be secured by the kings and states, with the knowledge and good will of the churches.

25. It could also be arranged for the prominent members or their delegates to meet in a certain place every ten or fifty years, to hold a world convention where they would all render an account of all things and tell how the followers of light, peace and the grace of God have increased in numbers, and finally to give stability to this ministering rule of Christ; lest here or there a new Antichrist should arise, trying to become a new prophet, a new head of the church, or a new monarch.

26. But let us consider the tasks of these colleges singly in order to make this flower of human pre-eminence the foundation and the pillar of all order in the world.

The universal bond between scholars, the College of Light.

It will be their task to direct relations between mind and being, that is to say, to guide human omniscience that it may not exceed its bounds nor fall short, nor err from its path, in any of its degrees, conditions or cases; to extend the dominion of the human mind over things and promote the light of wisdom among all nations and minds, always for the higher and better. This College could also be called the Teacher of the human race, the Heaven of the Church and the Luminary of the world.

2. They will have to pay attention

(i) To themselves, as the ministers to the Light;

(ii) To the Light itself, to be refined and diffused by their works;

(iii) To the schools, as the workshops of light;

(iv) To the heads of the schools, as the light-bearers;

(v) To teaching methods, as the purifiers of light;

(vi) To books, as the vessels of light;

(vii) To the printers, as the makers of these vessels;

(viii) To the new language, as the finest vehicle of the new light;

(ix) To the other two colleges, as assistants in spreading light everywhere;

(x) To Christ Himself, the fount of light.

Let us consider each of these spheres of attention separately.

3. They will pay attention to themselves first and foremost, to be themselves what they should make others: enlightened, first and foremost, like the true luminary of the world; like the moon, I say, whose light shall be as the light of the sun, and like the sun, whose light shall be sevenfold, as the light of seven days (Isaiah, xxx. 26); like Solon and Solomon, the wisest of mortals, whose wisdom, maker of all things, taught them all such things as are either secret or manifest (Wisdom, vii. 21); like libraries endowed with a soul, living temples of the Muses, true torches of God lit for the good of the whole world. Otherwise, if through neglect and indifference these light-bearers become clouded stars and luminaries eclipsed, what will become of the rest of the body of human society? Christ did not pass it over in silence, saying: 'If therefore the light that is in thee be darkness, how great is that darkness!' (Matthew, vi. 23).

4. Then they will pay attention to the light of wisdom itself, which they are to make shine in beauty over all the variety of things and their universality, to clarify and purify, and to spread effectively over all nations to the ends of the earth. For just as the sun in the sky was not born and given to any one region alone, but rises for all men, turning towards the south and back towards the north and lighting up all things around; so the sun of the mind, wisdom, rising already now with such splendour, should not belong to one or even to a few peoples, but should follow its orbit over the whole human race; these apostles of the light will see and provide for this; thus will they be the brightest lightbearers, bringing the light of the dawn to the darkness of the peoples of the world, until such time as the sun of justice Himself, Christ, shall rise. And wherever that sun has already risen, they will take care that no darkness of the mind should return to darken the daylight of the Church, that no little star of partial knowledge already shining in the firmament of the Church should cease to shine, and even less that the sun of the Church itself, or the moon, should decline; for the Lord shall be its everlasting light, as has been promised (Isaiah, IX. 20).

5. In the third place they will pay earnest attention to the workshops of light, the schools, that schools should be opened among all nations and all communities of human society, and that having been opened they are maintained, and being maintained that they are lit with perpetual light. For just as the sun fills its planets with its light and shines over the whole globe of the world (except for what turns away and seeks shade among the opaque bodies); so the light-bearers will enlighten all the schools as the orbit assigned to them. They will therefore urge all the heads of the church and the civic bodies to tolerate no house, no village, no town, no province in which learning and wisdom are not taught. That is to say that there should be an elementary school in every village and for every so many inhabitants; a grammar school in every city; a university in every kingdom. And in order that everything may be done as it should be,

teachers and tutors, curators and proctors should be permanently in attendance, and inspectors should come at certain times, preserving all things in good condition and reforming any errors which may have crept in.

6. Then they will have under their supervision the authorities in the schools, the teachers, masters, professors, rectors, curators and proctors; they must observe most attentively whether they all do all they should rightly, and endeavour to instruct those who are ignorant of their task, arouse the careless, and remove from office those who cannot be reformed; that nothing should be tolerated in these workshops of light but what is clear, ardent and pleasant.

7. In particular they will pay attention to the methods of teaching used by this, that or the other man in educating young people; whether they lead their charges to the fixed goal along the right road, over level ground, gently and pleasantly; or whether they still afflict them, dragging them by circuitous ways, along rough roads and over thorns. For even God Himself, taking pity on young people, has shown at last how all schools can be made into playgrounds; therefore we cannot suffer any school to continue to be like a grindstone or a house of torment for souls. Therefore that all schools should become gardens of delight, the members of the College of Light will pay the greatest attention to seeing that everything in school is achieved without coercive discipline, as far as possible, but not without it either, if the matter demands it; so that human nature is neither ruined by whipping Orbilioes nor weakened by indulgent and easy-going masters.

8. But a far broader field in which to employ their wisdom is opened to them by the care for books. It will be their task to see to it that: (1) no people and no language should be without books any more; (2) that the books should be good; (3) that the editions should be unadulterated, large enough and easily accessible; (4) that books should not lie about neglected as they have been up to the present, but that everybody should read and understand them; (5) that they should be corrected and

brought up to date according to the light that has been gained since; or that new books should be written, complete channels of the new light.

9. It will be their primary care, however, to see that as a symbol of the universal reign of Christ throughout the earth all nations should have His laws and ordinances printed, i.e., the Holy Bible: (1) in their own tongue; (2) in a correct version; (3) in a fair edition easily obtainable. For this is a greater matter than when Ahasuerus ordered his commands to be made known to all the peoples subject to his rule, in the language and the writing of each nation (Esther, VIII. 9). Aids from without are needed for the Spirit of God to inspire all men and speak to all men. The King of Spain issues his orders to his people in Spanish, the King of France in French, etc. Therefore let the Holy Spirit (Viceroy in the Church of Christ) speak to all peoples in all tongues, as He began at the beginning of the Gospel. Why should the mystery of salvation be taught only in the Latin tongue? It is not in this that the apostolic universal episcopy consists!

10. And since a foremost instrument in the reformation of the world are books, according to the words of the angel: 'When the world shall be finished, the books shall be opened before the firmament, and they shall see all together' (II Esdras, VI. 20); and since it is the printers that bring books into the world; this sphere also falls to the College of Light, to pay attention to them. They must consider what measures should be taken to avert dangers in the future, that in the days to come this art should be considered a sacred gift from God and one to be used only for the glory of God and the common benefit of the human race. This will be so if:

(i) Nobody is allowed to practise this craft without the permission of the authorities. It is certainly dangerous to entrust so great a matter to any chance person. For if the minting of money is reserved exclusively to the ruler and no private person is allowed to do it, although money is only the instrument for outward business; what measures should not be taken in such a matter as this, a thousand times more important and a thousand times more open to abuse? Nobody believes paper is made for anybody who likes to smear it as he will.

(ii) To this end let no man be a printer who is not appointed by the authorities and by the Church and by the College of Light, and let them be men of the greatest learning, wisdom, prudence and piety, and in addition let them be under oath, that the world may be protected from aberrations in this sphere in every possible way.

(iii) Nor can these workshops of light be allowed to exist clandestinely, or in any odd corner; but only there where those who profess the light live, in the universities, so that whatever issues forth, the very fact that it issues forth from this place should be sufficient testimony that it is a good thing; like public property accessible to the public, or like good gold or silver coins made in the public mint, it will be the public instrument for public trade in wisdom.

(iv) To make this matter even more secure and certain, let no one of the printers (however learned and pious a man, and under oath) publish anything according to his private judgement, relying on his own sagacity; but only what he is ordered to print by the public authorities, the king, princes, government, church, university, or the College of Light.

(v) Let no book be printed again, once it has been issued, without the knowledge of the same authorities; so that no opportunity of realizing anything to be added, deleted or emended should be neglected.

(vi) So much for the essentials. It will be an added advantage, and one which is worthy of an enlightened age, if great care is taken to see that in public books (and in future all books will be public) no printing errors are allowed to appear. Towards the end of the last century the famous Antwerp printer Plantinus enjoyed this fame, publishing books so accurately printed that it was considered amazing if there was a single error, even of a full stop, in any of his books. It is right for all printers to emulate this great diligence, for (1) it is a beautiful thing in itself, (2) it is useful to make the reader safe from error, even in the smallest things, and (3) it is possible, therefore, let it be done. It is certainly right that everything should be done as well as possible.

(vii) It will be easy to do this if (1) the texts are correct, clearly written, and read through again and again; (2) the typesetter is an educated young man with a thorough knowledge of spelling; (3) the same applies even more urgently to the proof-reader, who must be earnest and industrious, never letting himself doze. Or there may be two of them, the second of whom would receive a special premium for his vigilance, having sharper eyes. Plantinus himself took part in this work, looking through all proofs after the first correction, and then passing them on to the second proof-reader; if the latter still found any mistakes, Plantinus paid him a golden ducat for every one. Other incentives to diligence could also be used, such as the printing of the proof-reader's name at the end of the book, as we have seen them beginning to do in some books printed in Italy. Thus would the readers take care not to be nodding Homers, if they had to bear either public praise for their diligence or public disgrace for their negligence.

(viii) What I am about to say next may seem trivial, but it is part of the idea of the perfect reformation of things. If there should be nothing done without reason (and that without good reason), why do we see on the title pages of books and in the capital letters flowers, trees, little birds, serpents and what is worse, the most distorted monsters? Some writers and printers are coming to their senses, and not wishing to depart from the accepted practice in the design of letters, change it to something more rational; e.g., they draw Phaeton for the letter P, Elijah ascending into Heaven for the letter E, etc. The same is true of those who have started prefixing the titles of their books with pictures and symbols which foreshadow the theme of the whole book. This is a reasonable and beautiful practice, worthy of general imitation.

(ix) Finally the printers should be persuaded to leave the ranks of the craftsmen and associate with the learned, to carry out their divine task with a free and liberal mind.

11. Publishers must be requested and urged not to multiply pages, but wisdom; not taking as their goal the lucre of moneybags, but the enlightening of minds; that they may thus be true ministers of the light and not slaves of Pluto, creators of darkness and confusion. Let the members of the College of Light bear in mind that it is part of their supervision to see that this should not happen.

12. Since the finest vehicle of the new light is the new language, the members of the College of Light will consider it their duty to construct this language and spread it among the peoples, so that whatever new light on the new sciences, arts, crafts and inventions may arise in any corner of the world whatsoever, may become the common property of all peoples and nations; and relations between peoples all over the world not an instrument for visible profit, but primarily for the propagation of God's light among the peoples by the gift of the new language.

13. To this end they will be in friendly agreement with the other two tribunals, as with their helpers in the spreading the light over all things. They will also support the other tribunals actively with their sound advice, like smiths and grinders sharpening their hoes, ploughshares and sickles, and resolve whatever knotty problems arise between the theologians and the politicians, so that the ecclesiastical tribunal will be left only decisions on matters of conscience, and the political tribunal only questions of violence and the remedies for violence. In future let the writing of books be a matter not for politicians or for churchmen, but for the members of the College of Light; for theory belongs to the latter, and practice to the former. Therefore whatever is needful in the sphere of theory should be sought by both churchmen and politicians from the College of Light. On the other hand, the latter will put nothing before the public without having had it tried in practice by both the others, and without their opinion and

approval. Let the politicians wield the sceptre and give all their attention to the question of peace; let the theologians administer the Word, the keys and the sacraments, and give all their attention to keeping man's soul close to God. In this way their duties will not be confused.

14. The sum of all these things is that they should serve Christ, the light of the soul and of the peoples, that the nations should walk in His light—that at the evening time of the world the light may be clear, not like the twilight which went before (Zechariah, xvi), and that the earth may be filled with the light of knowledge, as the waters cover the sea.

The universal bond between States, the Dicastery of Peace

It will be their task to watch over human wisdom in governing themselves through all degrees and conditions, or even cases (which may happen) to maintain undisturbed human society with all its business, on all sides. In other words, to lead the propagation of justice and peace from nation to nation all over the world. It could be called the Directorate of the powers of the world, the Senate of the earth, or the Areopagus of the world; the directors themselves could be best called the Eirenarchs of the kingdoms (the supreme arbiters of peace); Cicero called the Roman Senate *orbis terrae consilium,* but the name would be more appropriate for this Dicastery of the world.

2. Going into greater detail, their tasks will be to pay strict attention to:

(i) Themselves, as the criterion and example of justice;

(ii) Justice itself, in all ranks of human society;

(iii) In particular the courts of justice and institutions of government, as the seat of justice;

(iv) Judges, as the priests of justice;

(v) The juridical procedure employed by this man or that;

(vi) The laws or the books setting out the law;

(vii) The interpreters of the laws, the commentators and notaries;

(viii) Measures, weights, coins, public ways, etc., as instruments of public equity and security;

(ix) The other two tribunals, as helpers in guarding order;

(x) Finally God Himself, the eternal defender of justice.

Each of these must be considered separately in turn.

3. Their first duty will be to be themselves first and foremost such as they are to teach others to be: just on all sides, peace-loving, pleasant, loyal; a true bond binding human society, true magnets drawing all men and all things to the pole of peace, living columns and supports of all order in the human race; Melchizedek come to life again, kings of justice; Solomon come to life again, kings of peace; Moses come to life again, diligent to reconcile fraternal disputes; the mildest of men, perhaps even the most heavily burdened with labours, and the strongest to suffer all things, altogether a lion's nature.

4. But it will not be enough for them to set an example of adamantine loyalty and to instil the love for it into all other men; they must pay attention to the way the counsels of peace are universally followed. Thus they will be the foremost defenders of the common weal, to prevent wars, tumults and bloodshed from returning, or the occasion for them; that all such things should rather be buried in eternal oblivion. Standing thus on the lookout they will not stand watch only over the peace of one nation, or each only over his own, but over the peace of the whole world, building eternal barriers to war everywhere, that before the world comes to an end the primaeval state of the world may return, peaceful in all ways, as Christ (Luke, XVII. 26, 27) and the Apostle (I Thessalonians, v. 3) prophesied.

5. In the third place they will turn their attention, to this end, to the public workshops for the preservation of peace, the courts of government, the tribunals of law, the assemblies; that these may be set up in every nation

for the administration of justice, for the prevention of injustice, quarrels and conflicts, or for their early settlement should any arise anywhere; so that nobody may be left without refuge, defence and protection, if he suffers injury or fears it. To this end they will also pursue this special task: if any nation by God's blessing has so multiplied and is so hard-pressed by reason of its numbers that the native soil is not enough for all, it will be the task of the Eirenarchs to foresee this and take steps in time, so that the people do not seek their relief at the expense of others, as they have done up to now, unrestrainedly attacking their fellows or their neighbours, driving them out and killing them; but rather by founding colonies elsewhere so that all may live well, and thus fulfil the laws of charity and at the same time fill the earth with concord. This should not be done haphazardly and by force (as the Spaniards, Portuguese, French, English, Belgians and others did not long ago) but following the example of Abraham with Lot (Genesis, XIII. 8) using arbiters of peace.

6. The Eirenarchs will see to it that the public judges are such as the state of public peace requires, forming and strengthening them all to their own pattern (as has been said in paragraph 3). Let none of them tolerate anything irrational in the jurisdiction of his circuit, but teach and force all men to live together in humane fashion, and that rather by preventing than by punishing offences, troubles and damage done. For if anything should happen which could give occasion for discord, such as arguments over boundaries, etc., they will teach and admonish the people not to lower their human dignity by starting hatred and litigation for material things. For it is fitting for man to act according to reason, or if a matter of doubt arises, to try to judge, but not to act in passion or in anger, with force or arms; that is akin to the animals and cannot be tolerated any longer.

7. They will also consider by what means peace and tranquillity could be preserved throughout all human society without the use of violent measures, as far as pos-

sible; without prisons, swords, nooses, gallows, etc., that
the holy government of Christ's kingdom be not stained
with executions; but if any man is determined to be ob-
durate in the extreme, it will be their task to seek and
find means of subduing this indomitable malice so that
it cannot cause public harm.

8. But to make it possible to be without this kind of
extreme violence they will take steps to have written
down all cases which cause trouble to human society, together with the remedies to be applied to each in good
time; that it will no longer be so easy to disturb the
peace in any nation, city or house. It has been thought
that this has already been done, since laws and statutes
have long been made and passed by states and munici-
palities; but it was but partial, more often serving custom than immutable standards of law, and never perhaps sufficient for all cases. Universal law must therefore
be established, to serve the whole of the human race in
all cases. It will be drawn only from the laws of nature
and the laws of God, and will therefore be binding on
all who partake of human nature and the divine light.
They will also note laws which are doubtful, and offer
general advice about them; and also laws which are obviously injurious and to be abolished for ever (Isaiah,
LXVI. 2, 4). The Eirenarchs of the world, the supreme
advocates of peace, will not cease to urge and press the
scholars to write such books, immutable standards of
law and justice, until that which is desired comes to
pass indeed. They will also see to it that these laws are so
well known to all men, like their own fingers, that no
man can transgress under pretext of ignorance.

9. To this end they will have lesser inspectors of the
law under them, and to them they will recommend
these standards of law and justice, that they may direct
all execution of the law according to them. And once a
year, taking with them one or two serious men, they will
visit all the courts of law and see for themselves how the
law is carried out by this man or that; they will confirm those that work well, admonish those that err, and
thus preserve the right course in all things.

10. These supreme heads of administration and peace will make particular efforts by their authority, favour and active support to help, support and maintain in vigour the other two tribunals; they will see to it that the authority of the ministers of the church, especially the members of the Consistory, is safe in every way and no less that the lights of the world, especially the members of the College of Light, can carry out their tasks of enlightening the world without impediment. Thus they will ensure the means of procuring good books and other essential things, their distribution among the nations and their proper use; that is to say, they will gain favour, urgency and the necessary money.

11. But the highest goal the Eirenarchs of the world will set themselves will be to defend the cause of the King of Kings, that beneath his peaceful sceptre all the sceptres of the world may reign in peace, and that all the crowns of the kingdoms of the world may be laid before the throne of God and the Lamb. This will come to pass if every one of the rulers is content with that portion of government which has fallen to his lot by valid election or by heredity; let him not go beyond this nor disturb the rule of others in their own sphere. The right to rule over all things belongs to no man but the new Adam, Christ, to whom the Father gave all rights over the whole world lost by the first Adam. If then any man seek to rule over all things, he is seeking Babylon, bringing confusion into the world again. But he that builds the kingdom of Christ is building Sion, the rule of the saints. And so these guardians of the public weal will keep watch lest the kingdom of Antichrist, once destroyed, and the remnants of the wild beasts prowling the earth, should return again, and will put a curse on any who would try to build up again the cursed city of Jericho (Jeremiah, xvi. 6). The Lord of Heaven and earth will confirm the word of His servants, laying a curse upon the house of Hiel, although he was of Bethel itself, i.e., of the very house of God (I Kings, xvi. 34).

12. Thus at last will come fulfilment of so many prayers and supplications addressed to God the Father

by the whole church for so many ages: 'Thy kingdom come, Thy will be done, in earth as it is in Heaven'; fulfilment not of itself (for this is not the work of man) but by Him who makes all things good, in His own time, and who carries out His ordinary work in an ordinary way. Blessed are they who give themselves to Him as a tool. Seeking the kingdom of God and His justice they will find the kingdom of God; and under the reign of Christ (whom God the Father has ordered to reign) they will reign with Him over all lands (Apocalypse, v. 10), and this kingdom will be the kingdom of the saints (Daniel, VII. 22, 27). Long live the King of Peace! Long live His kingdom in peace! from now and for ever more! Amen, Hallelujah! Amen, Hallelujah! Amen, Hallelujah!

A Proposal for an International
Education Center

MARC-ANTOINE JULLIEN

*The following selection is the only work of Jullien's
which was published in the United States during
his life. His pamphlet,* Esquisse et Vues Préliminaires d'un Ouvrage sur L'Éducation Comparée, *is
not available for reprinting, but this selection sum-
marizes Jullien's views and lists some of the questions he proposed as a scheme of inquiry for the
initial steps in the establishment of an international
bureau of education.*

M. M.–A. JULLIEN'S QUESTIONS ON
COMPARATIVE EDUCATION.*

A FRIEND has favored us with a French pamphlet under
the following title

*Esquisse et Vues Préliminaires d'un ouvrage sur L'
Éducation Comparée, &c.*

The author M. M.–A. Jullien of Paris, holds a distinguished rank among the literary and scientific men of
his country. He has devoted a more persevering and systematic attention to the subject of education, than perhaps any other individual of our day. The substance of
his pamphlet which we have mentioned above, has appeared in the *Journal D' Éducation,* a work published under the auspices of the Paris Society for the Improvement of Elementary Instruction.†

The author's object in the pamphlet from which the
following extracts are made, is to present a preliminary
sketch of a great work, designed to embrace a comparative view of the actual state of education throughout Eu-

* *American Journal of Education,* Vol. I (July, 1826), pp. 408ff.
† For an account of this society see intelligence Nos. 1 and 2 of
this Journal [*American Journal of Education*].

53

rope. He commences by expressing a well founded regret that there is a great want of connection, harmony, and proportion, in the grand departments of physical, moral, and intellectual education, as hitherto conducted. He then suggests the advantages likely to arise from a work which might offer the results of a diligent and thorough investigation of the present state of the various establishments for education in Europe—whether elementary and common, secondary and classical, superior and scientific, or special. Of this classification the first branch corresponds to our common schools, the second to academies, and other preparatory seminaries, the third to colleges, the fourth to professional institutions.

The schools of Pestalozzi and Fellenberg are mentioned with commendation, as auspicious to improvement, also the polytechnic school of Paris, and the Lancasterian schools in England.

The attention of the sovereigns of Europe is invited to the formation of a special Commission of Education, to be composed of a few individuals who might chuse corresponding members at a distance, and proceed to the great work of compiling an account of the state of education.

M. Jullien suggests, further, the establishment of a Normal Institute of Education, for the instruction of teachers, under the most favorable circumstances for personal and professional improvement.

He recommends a Bulletin or Journal of Education, arranged under the same number of heads as might be adopted in the inquiries of the Special Commission already mentioned. These inquiries would be guided by the scheme of questions which forms the principal part of the author's pamphlet.

The following are the leading topics of this department of the work

Education.—1st. its *subject.*—2d. its *object.*—3d. its *instrument.*

1. The (*subject,*) MAN—as composed of *three* elements: the *body,*—the *heart,* (the affections,)—the *intellect.*

2. (The *object* of education,) *Happiness*—as consisting in *three* things: *health,*—*virtue,*—*instruction.*

3. (The *instrument* of education,) TIME as divided into *infancy, boyhood, youth.*

The series of questions which follow are arranged under the principal heads of

Schools, 1st, Elementary, primary, and common.

2d. Secondary and classical.

3d. Superior and scientific and professional.

Three other series of questions are comprehended under

4. Normal schools.

5. Schools for females.

6. Public schools.

Subdivision of the First Series, Education primary and common. 1. Schools.—2. Teachers.—3. Pupils.—4. Physical and gymnastic education.—5. Moral and religious education.—6. Intellectual instruction.—7. Connection between domestic and private, and public education.—8. Connection between primary and secondary schools.—9. General considerations, and miscellaneous questions.

These nine topics are applied with suitable modifications to secondary and classical schools, and the others which are mentioned.

We return to the questions under the head of

PRIMARY EDUCATION.

Schools.

1. What is the number of elementary or primary schools in the town, district, canton, province, &c.?

2. What is the nature, and what are the names of the schools, as German, French, &c. week-day or Sunday, common to the two sexes or restricted to one; common to all children in the same place, or appropriated to the poor, to the rich, to the middle class?

3. At what date was each school founded? Who were the founders?

4. How are these schools supported—at the expense and under the charge of the central government, of each community, or of particular societies, or of revenues

arising from endowments? How are the funds administered by which they are supported?

5. What are the buildings appropriated to these schools —more or less spacious, commodious, airy, and adapted to their object? (The places where children are brought up during their first years, exercise a powerful influence on their imagination, and the developement of all their faculties.)

6. What are the circles which these schools embrace— a town or only part of a town, a parish, a borough, a village, or one or more hamlets?

7. In what proportion is the number of these schools to the town, circle, district, &c. in which they are established, and to the whole number of children who attend them?

8. Are there distinct schools for children whose parents are of different religious communions; and what is the proportion between the schools of each communion?

9. If there are distinct schools for children of different religious communions, what difference can be remarked between these schools in regard to their origin and foundation, their organisation and their maintenance, material, (of which the buildings are constructed) site, administration, and expenses, number of pupils proportioned to that of the inhabitants professing the same religion, choice of instructers, instruction and progress of the children, internal discipline, and external superintendence.

10. Are the schools gratuitous or not, or what is the monthly or yearly sum paid for each child?

11. What are the terms of admission to the primary schools?

12. Do all the parents send their children to these schools, and are they invited or obliged by legislative measures, or by local regulations to send them?

Primary Instructers.

13. What pains are taken to form good instructers of primary schools?

14. What are the conditions of age, country, religion, morality, capacity, which are required for such employment?

15. How, and by what authorities or corporations, or by what individuals, are the nominations made?

16. What is the number of instructers in the town, circle, district, &c.?

17. In what proportion is the number of these instructers to the whole population of the town, &c.?

18. In what proportion to the total number of pupils, and to the pupils in each school?

19. What are the names of the instructers who distinguish themselves most in their employment? What is their age? How long have they been in employment?

20. Generally, do teachers who are young, or those who are more advanced in age, succeed better?

21. Is it the duty of instructers of primary schools to give at fixed periods an account of the condition of the classes which they superintend—of the conduct and the progress of the children?—At what periods, in what form, under what particular relation, are these accounts demanded, and to whom are they addressed? What means are taken to ascertain their correctness?

22. What are the annual salaries of primary instructers? Are these salaries invariably fixed, or casual, and dependent on the number of children?—What is their maximum—What their minimum? What indemnities or particular advantages are allowed them, independently of their fixed salary? Are they properly provided with lodging, airy, light, and warm? Do they receive a certain portion of grain, of wine, or of other provisions? At what sum may these supplements to salary or indemnities be valued?

23. How, at what periods, and on what funds, are these salaries, principal or subsidiary?

24. Have primary instructers the prospect of a progressive advancement of their salary, or of an advance at a certain stage of their career—whether at the end of a certain number of years of service, or on the ground of their talents or their zeal, or the increase in the num-

ber of their pupils? On what foundation rests this aug-
mentation of salary or this promotion? By whom is it
proposed, determined, granted? In what does it consist?

25. Have they also the prospect of securing a retreat,
after a certain number of years' service? What is the number of years? What is the amount of such pension? By
whom is it granted and fixed?

26. In case of accidents or infirmities which may
oblige an instructer to retire before the time stipulated
for a pension, can he at least obtain an indemnity proportioned to the duration and the benefit of his services?

27. Have primary instructers a sufficient guaranty for
the preservation of their places, and are they never ex-
posed to an arbitrary destitution?

28. If faulty conduct or discovered incapacity makes it
necessary to displace an instructer, how and by whom, is
the arrangement ordered?

29. Do instructers enjoy a degree of consideration
sufficient to render their condition honorable?

30. What are their habitual relations with the parents
of their pupils, with the magistrates of their town, with
the ministers of religion?

Pupils.

31. What is the number of the pupils in the primary
schools of the district, &c.?

32. What is the proportion of the whole number of
those pupils to that of the population of the district, &c.

33. What number of pupils is under the charge of the
same instructer?

34. At what age are children admitted to the primary
schools?

35. Are children of both sexes admitted into the same
school, and till what age?

36. Do children undergo, on their entering the primary school, and during their elementary course, examinations suited to produce an estimation of the developement of their faculties, and the progress of their
instruction. How do these examinations take place?

37. Is care taken to divide the children of the same

school into several classes or sections, and on what basis is this division determined?

38. Are arrangements made which permit the children to aid themselves, and instruct themselves mutually?

39. How much time is employed with an ordinary child, to render him familiar with the elements of reading, writing, and calculation?

40. At what age do children leave the primary schools?

Education Physical and Gymnastic.

41. For how long a time are infants in general nursed in the country—in the city?

42. What kind of nourishment is given to some infants instead of the milk of their mothers, and what effects do these aliments produce on the health of children?

43. Do the wealthier citizens commit their infants to nurses or do the mothers themselves attend to the office of nursing.

44. How are infants nourished after being weaned? Till what age are they hindered from eating meat, and drinking wine?

45. What clothing is used for infants?

46. Is it customary to clothe infants slightly, in all seasons; or are they kept warmly clad?

47. How many hours are children permitted to sleep, till they have attained the age of six or eight years; and how are the hours of repose distributed?

48. Are the beds of children hard, in order to invigorate their bodies, or are they soft; and of what are they ordinarily composed?

49. During sleep, is the head covered or bare, and on what ground is a preference given to either practice?

50. Till what age, in cities, do children usually remain under the care of females, and what are the observations made regarding children who have been put under the charge of men, earlier than comports with common usage?

51. What attention is given to fortifying children by accustoming them early to the open air, and to cold— and by enuring them to fatigue?

52. What are the ordinary sports of children—whether in the family or at school?

53. Are they accustomed to long walks—before or after eating?

54. What success is there in directing and superintending—in an indirect manner without infringing the liberty of children—their exercises and their sports?

55. By what exercises are children rendered agile? Are they taught to use both hands equally?

56. Are they frequently bathed in cold water—lake or river—or in warm baths?

57. Are they taught to swim, and at what age? What precautions are used to prevent accidents?

58. What pains are taken about cleanliness and neatness?

59. What are the rules of hygiene (the preservation and promotion of health) generally followed with children?

60. Are the children generally healthy, strong, and robust?

61. What are the maladies most common among children?

62. Does the small pox still exist, and is it destructive?

63. Is vaccination generally adopted; and for how long a time has the practice existed?

64. How many infants generally are in one year affected with severe illness, and of what kind?

65. What is the proportion of mortality among children under ten years of age?

(Well educated and experienced physicians, and intelligent magistrates, are referred to as proper persons from whom to receive answers to most of the preceding questions.)

The author of the pamphlet from which we have translated the foregoing passages, did not anticipate for his work a wider sphere of usefulness, than it might find in Europe. But there seems to be no good reason why his efforts should not extend their influence to America. The very perusal of his questions, will, we think, do much good everywhere. We shall pursue them farther in a future number.

Education at the Peace Conference*

FANNIE FERN ANDREWS

The failure of the League of Nations to include education among its responsibilities curtailed the entire movement for international education for several decades. Fannie Fern Andrews, who had led the movement for an international bureau in the years immediately preceding World War I, describes, in the following essay, the results of a meeting held by those interested in education with the delegates who wrote the Covenant of the League.

The force of education in promoting intelligent partnership among the nations and in creating a common motive for democratic progress has long been recognized by those engaged in the instruction of youth. When the delegates at the Peace Conference began to work out a draft for a League of Nations, educational thinkers became active in formulating plans whereby education can perform its full service to this momentous undertaking. They based their efforts on the assumption that the permanent stability of such a League depends primarily upon the aims and methods of the educational system of the nations that comprise the League. A definite proposition was presented to the League of Nations Commission—that of creating a permanent bureau or commission of education as part of the organization of the League. This request came from several different sources. The first definite resolution was passed by the meeting of delegates of allied associations for a Society of Nations held at Paris from the twenty-fifth to the thirtieth of January, under the presidency of Leon

* American School Citizenship League, *An Eleven-Year Survey of the Activities of the American School Peace League* (Boston, 1919), pp. 7-10.

Bourgeois. This resolution declared that: an international commission of education should be an active organ in a League of Free Nations. Education is the principal means by which a responsible world democracy may be evolved and a League of Nations maintained. The International Commission on Education should be entrusted to draw up a plan, whereby education will promote the fundamental needs of democracy. This plan, therefore, should provide for a widespread education in the elements of democratic citizenship and the extension of the privilege of education to all peoples and classes.

Almost simultaneously with this, the United States Army Educational Commission sent a memorandum to the League of Nations Commission, stating at some length the part that education might play in a League of Nations. This was followed by the endorsement of a commission on education, in the form of resolutions, by the General Education Board and the Department of Superintendence of the National Education Association of the United States.

The Workers' Educational Association, representing over twenty-seven hundred educational, working-class, and other associations in Great Britain and Ireland, sent a strong resolution to the Commission declaring among other things that the attitude of mind "essential to the successful and effective working of a democratic League of Peoples . . . can only be cultivated by education that aims at enlightening the peoples of the world as to the facts of the world they live in, more especially the social and the economic facts that periodically divide the human family into warring communities, widens the human outlook, broadens and deepens human sympathies, and enables the democracies of the world to realize their interdependence on each other for their future prosperity and security.

"On behalf of the Workers' Educational Association, which represents 2,709 educational, working-class, and other organizations in Great Britain and Ireland, we therefore urge that the League of Nations Commission set up an International Commission on Education, for we regard such a commission as essential to the successful and effective working of a democratic League of Peoples."

The National Union of Teachers of Great Britain, and the Educational Section of the British League of Nations Union sent equally strong endorsements.

The International Council of Women and Conference of Women Suffragists of the Allied Countries and of the United States presented the following resolutions to the League of Nations Commission when that body formally received the delegation on April 10, and listened to addresses supporting this and other resolutions presented on the same occasion:

> WHEREAS a League of Nations should be not only an instrument of peace but also an instrument of civilization;
>
> WHEREAS for the maintenance of a League of Nations it is essential to teach children from an early age to understand its usefulness and its benefits and to respect its aims;
>
> WHEREAS the true freedom of men and women can only be gained by a liberal and democratic education, open to all citizens alike:
>
> The International Council of Women and the Conference of Women Suffragists of the Allied Countries and the United States petition as follows:
>
> THAT a provision be made in the covenant of the League of Nations for an International Bureau of Education.

The following article was proposed for insertion in the final Covenant of the League of Nations:

> The High Contracting Parties will endeavor to make the aims and methods of their educational systems consistent with the general principles underlying the League of Nations; and to this end agree to establish as part of the organization of the League a permanent bureau of education.

This international organ presents no new idea. Before the war, the International Federation of National Associations of Teachers, representing some twenty different States, endorsed the idea of an International Bureau of Education.

Moreover, the governments of seventeen states, in 1913, appointed delegates to the International Conference on Education which was called by the Netherlands government at the suggestion of the government of the United States for September, 1914. The call to this Conference contained a Draft Convention for an International Bureau of Education.

The Covenant of the League of Nations does not contain the provision for a Bureau of Education, but this does not signify hostility to the subject. On the contrary several of the members of the League of Nations Commission have individually expressed great interest. As President Wilson said, when the various resolutions were presented to the commission on April 10:

> If we do not include all the measures which you have proposed, it is not because we are not in sympathy with them, but that we think it is wise to confine ourselves merely to the setting up of the framework of the League of Nations, leaving the complete organization for future development.

Our great duty to-day is to create enthusiasm for the League of Nations; and as this becomes a working institution, the need of some definite and direct means of fostering the spirit which inspired its creation will become more and more apparent. This viewpoint should be pressed, for the success of the League of Nations will depend on a world outlook which can only be achieved through a systematic and conscious education of the peoples.

Part II INTERNATIONAL ORGANIZATION

-→>※<<-

The International Committee on Intellectual Cooperation*

Within a short time after the founding of the League of Nations, constant demand by various scientific organizations and associations concerned with humanities led to the proposal of a special "Committee to examine international questions regarding intellectual cooperation." The following report of proceedings leading to the formation of the Committee includes an account of the unsuccessful motion by M. Bellegarde, delegate from Haiti, to make "education" a function of the Committee.

REPORT OF COMMITTEE NO. 5 ON THE INTERNATIONAL ORGANISATION OF INTELLECTUAL WORK.

*   *   *

Professor Gilbert MURRAY, rapporteur, read the following report:

"The Committee appointed by the Second Assembly to consider the problem of the organisation of intellectual work sat on September 8th and 10th. It had before it the report of M. Léon Bourgeois, adopted by the Council on September 2nd, 1921, and two memoranda by the Secretary-General: (1) on the educational activities and the co-ordination of intellectual work accomplished by the Union of International Associations (A. 42 *(b)*, 1921); and (2) on the desirability of creating a technical organisation (A. 42 *(c)*, 1921).

* *The Records of the Second Assembly, Plenary Meeting* (Geneva, The League, 1921), pp. 309-314.

65

"The discussion was introduced by M. Lafontaine.

"The Committee considered the desirability of sending the question to a special sub-committee, but decided that the highly complex and technical nature of the problems involved made it unlikely that such a course would be profitable.

"The Committee realises the great importance of the organisation of intellectual work; it knows that the future of the League of Nations depends upon the formation of a universal conscience. This can only be created and developed if the scholars, the thinkers, and the writers in all countries maintain close mutual contact, and spread from one country to another the ideas which can ensure peace among the peoples, and if the efforts already made in this direction receive encouragement.

"After some discussion of the subjects to be included under the head of the organisation of intellectual work, the Committee decided to follow in principle the plan recommended in M. Bourgeois' report to the Council (Annex, p. 74).

"It was resolved:

> " 'That this Committee approves the draft resolution put forward by M. Léon Bourgeois in the name of the Council, namely, the nomination by the Council of a Committee to examine international questions regarding intellectual co-operation, this Committee to consist of not more than twelve members, and to contain both men and women.'

"It will be observed that the wording is not identical with that of the draft resolution in M. Bourgeois' report. There is both an omission and an addition. The words 'and education' have been omitted after 'intellectual co-operation.' On the other hand, a provision has been added that women should be included on the Committee."

Professor Gilbert MURRAY then added: This whole subject of the international organisation of intellectual work suffers, I think, from a certain vagueness, or at least it causes a difficulty in some minds as to its exact meaning. That is one of the reasons—perhaps the principal one—why we have thought it necessary to recommend the appointment of this expert Committee. I would venture to suggest that the work of this Committee will be to analyse the whole field, to see if the work suggested is really important, to see what part of it is strictly relevant to the work of the League and also to consider if it is likely to involve great expense. International action for the co-ordination of intellectual work will fall, I think, under three heads: (1) international action for the protection of the intellectual worker; (2) international action for the practical advance of knowledge; (3) a more remote, but fully as important, subject —international action with a view to the spread of the international spirit of the consciousness of human brotherhood.

As to the first point—action for the protection of the intellectual worker—that is clearly necessary. Since the war, especially, there has been a pheonomenon occurring in many societies which is fraught with very considerable danger. The manual workers are, to some extent, very fortunately able, by means of their political power, to secure their own situation, but the intellectual worker has often, in many cases which will occur to you, been reduced to a condition of great penury and distress. Now, in every country there are societies for protecting the intellectual worker, societies of authors, of dramatists, of teachers and the like. The question we have to consider is whether we can do anything to internationalise the action of those societies.

Secondly, there is the question of international action for the practical advance of knowledge. The interchange of results between individual scientific workers and separate societies goes on, of course, habitually all over the world. It has been grievously interrupted owing to the war and owing to the economic conditions which have succeeded the war. I think it is a suitable question for that Committee to consider whether any action by the

League can help towards the resumption of those relations.

Thirdly, there is the spread of the international spirit. Here we come at once upon that monument of international industry which we owe to M. Lafontaine and M. Otlet—the Centre Internationale, established at Brussels. This will be a record of international activities, a clearing-house for such activities, and a store-house of international information.

We come also upon the question of an international university. In a sense, all universities are international. Science, of course, does not recognise the boundaries of nationalism, and mathematics knows no country. But this university is international in a special sense. It studies the international bearings and relations of subjects which are studied by themselves in the ordinary universities. It is not yet a university; it is little more than an organisation of summer gatherings. It is obvious that a great work has to be done, not perhaps by the League, but, on the other hand, not entirely without the co-operation of the League, in counteracting the nationalist tendencies which have invaded education in almost every country.

This is one of the great dangers that lie before humanity in the future.

It is a great danger if any one nation concentrates its intellectual effort and directs the minds of its young people entirely upon its own glory and its own interests. That danger is, I am afraid, in different degrees, quite a real one in many countries. In fact, we do find in most countries in the ordinary education given that there is traditionally—not through anybody's fault, but merely as a result of tradition—an inculcation into the minds of the young of a somewhat excessive sense of the military glories of that particular country, a somewhat excessive interest in their own wars and in their own differences from their neighbours. We find sometimes instilled into the mind the germs of contempt for other nations. That is pure poison, of course, from our point of view. It is not patriotism; it is something we must try with all tact and caution in different countries—each in his own country—to eradicate. In England and America there has been a great attempt to reconsider the teaching of history in the schools, not so as to falsify history or to carry into execution any form of propaganda, but to bring the idea of the League of Nations into the minds of the teachers and the taught. This is taking place, not only in America and England, but in one form or another in many countries. It may be possible, or not possible, for the League of Nations in some way to take advantage of this movement and give it help. That is the kind of question which this Committee will have to consider.

There are many more subjects which I need not dwell upon. I think everybody will agree with me that they are important, and that they are intimately connected with the success of the League, and, I would venture to say, with the future hopes of mankind. On the other hand, I think anyone may very justly say that hardly a single one of them is suitable for the direct action of the League of Nations.

The Committee will be able to consider what part of all this activity is in any way definitely relevant to our work, and what sort of assistance or countenance we can give to the work that is being done in various nations which seems to us to point in the direction in which we ourselves wish the world to move.

For these reasons, Committee No. 5 agrees with M. Bourgeois that the subject should be studied by a specialist committee.

The number of members of the Committee, it has been suggested, should be twelve, but I think that a smaller number than twelve might be sufficient. The expenditure will be very slight, and when the Committee has reported we shall, I think, be able to learn the real conditions of this problem, and no longer be in danger, when we are dealing with it, of merely beating the air.

M. BELLEGARDE (Haiti).

Translation:

Mr. President, ladies and gentlemen, I must crave your indulgence for speaking at such a late hour. I have only a few brief remarks to make dealing with the suppression of the words "and education", which are in the text of the report originally submitted by M. Léon Bourgeois to the Council of the League of Nations.

I should like to have these words re-inserted, because it seems to me that questions of education should hold the foremost place in our efforts.

I did not have the pleasure of being present at the discussions of Committee No. 5, and consequently I do not know what considerations led them to come to that decision, but I have read rapidly the minutes published, and I note that the Committee has been careful to avoid the reproach of intervening in the domestic affairs of nations with regard to education.

It appears to me that this is entirely beside the point. What is our object in forming this Committee, which will have to deal with all international questions of intellectual co-operation? Our object is to collect for the information of all countries the results achieved by the human intellect. Now, if it is desired to co-ordinate the achievements of the human mind, how can we afford to neglect the formation of the human mind?

There can be no doubt that education tends more and more to become a scientific question. I admit that it is not for the League of Nations to give directions or to prescribe to each State the best methods of education to be adopted, but it seems to me that it is of capital importance for all the nations to be kept informed of the progress arrived at by the various peoples in the sphere of education.

In one of those slightly bombastic formulæ at which the disrespectful irony of our age is wont to smile, Victor Hugo said: "All men are mankind." The great poet affirmed thereby the universality and permanence of the characteristics of the human soul. It is obvious that methods of education must vary in different States, because all nations are anxious to develop along the lines of their national traditions; but it is none the less true that the human soul is one, and that methods of education which aim at the development of all our faculties may be applied to all men irrespective of nationality.

Exchange of information with regard to the efforts made by the various nations in the field of education is undoubtedly of considerable value, and I move, therefore,

> *That the Assembly restore the words "and education" to the text of the motion before us.*

I should like to add that I am extremely gratified to observe that the Committee has decided that women shall be allowed to sit on the Committee. In every sphere of human activity, women have acquired a place which no one present would dream of contesting, and, more especially in educational matters, they exercise a considerable influence, for psychological reasons which I need not develop here.

I consider that the words "and education," which are in the original draft by M. Léon Bourgeois, should be restored because it is extremely important for us, with a view to the formation of that international spirit of which Professor Gilbert Murray has just spoken, that an exchange of information should take place with regard to the pedagogic work carried out all over the world, so that we may arrive at that unity in varied form which we are endeavouring to achieve in this institution. (*Applause.*)

The PRESIDENT.

Translation:

The motion before the Assembly is an amendment, according to which the words "and education" be interpolated after the words "of intellectual co-operation."

Professor Gilbert MURRAY, rapporteur.—Ladies and gentlemen, I think we are in the presence of a slight misunderstanding. I agree, as far as I follow them, with the remarks of the delegate for Haiti, but the Committee left out the word "education" for one principal motive, and perhaps for a second subsidiary motive.

The principal motive was that, as we looked at the resolution, some members of the Committee formed the idea, rightly or wrongly, that the resolution in that form might possibly convey the impression that the League of Nations wanted to map out a scheme of education, and impose it on the different nations. We all felt that that would be a perfectly untenable proposition, and a thing to which we did not wish to give cognisance. Some of the Committee then considered, if we left out the word "education," whether the League might be taken as having no interest in the improvement of educational methods, or in the sort of movement I dwelt upon just now, going on in England and America, of trying to get the League of Nations into our text-books, and trying to remove some of the military enthusiasm from our text-books. Of course, we wanted to include that possible action, and if educational improvement is thought out in some countries, we should be very glad that it should be considered in other countries. Then the people who felt that the League of Nations must take some cognisance of education considered, I think quite rightly, that the very broad phrase "co-operation in intellectual work" certainly included education among its other activities, and that if the Committee emphasized education, it might seem as if we wanted the League to interfere in educational systems. That we entirely laid on one side. With all the other ideas suggested by M. Bellegarde the Committee would be in sympathy, and I venture to ask him, after that explanation, if he will withdraw his amendment.

The PRESIDENT.

Translation:

May I ask M. Bellegarde if he considers Professor Murray's explanation satisfactory, or whether he insists on his amendment?

M. BELLEGARDE (Haiti).

Translation:

In view of the explanation furnished by Professor Murray, I do not insist that my motion should be discussed and put to the Assembly.

It is understood, nevertheless, that education considered as a science should be added to the list of questions submitted to the expert committee. (*Assent.*)

The PRESIDENT.

Translation:

M. Bellegarde therefore withdraws his amendment.
M. Hanotaux will address the Assembly.

M. HANOTAUX (France).

Translation:

I presume it is quite understood that the motion before the Assembly consists solely of the conclusions of the report submitted to the Assembly by Committee No. 5? The other remarks are quite interesting, but of a purely personal nature, and the Assembly need only vote on the motion as it is framed with the amendment proposed by the Committee.

The PRESIDENT.

That is quite so, Sir.

If there are no other speakers, I will put the motion to the vote.

Does any member desire a vote by roll-call?

As no member requires a vote by roll-call, the vote will take place by heads of delegations rising in their seats.

The following is the text of the resolution before the Assembly:

RESOLUTION

"*The Assembly approves the draft resolution put forward by M. Léon Bourgeois in the name of the*

Council—namely, the nomination by the Council of a Committee to examine international questions regarding intellectual co-operation, this Committee to consist of not more than twelve members and to contain both men and women."

(A vote was taken by heads of delegations rising in their seats.)

(The resolution was adopted unanimously.)

ANNEX

TO THE FIFTEENTH MEETING.

The Organisation of Intellectual Work.

Resolution, presented by M. Léon Bourgeois, French Representative, adopted by the Council on September 2nd, 1921.

The Assembly calls upon the Council to appoint a Committee to examine international questions regarding intellectual co-operation and education. This Committee will consist of not more than twelve members, appointed by the Council. It will submit to the next Assembly a report on the measures to be taken by the League to facilitate intellectual exchange between nations, particularly as regards the communication of scientific information and methods of education.

Pending the consideration of this report by the Assembly, this Committee will act as an advisory organ to the Council, which may submit to it any technical questions of this kind arising before the next session of the Assembly.

To this Committee will also be assigned the task of examining a scheme for an International Office of Education, referred to in the Council's report dated March 1st, 1921.

The International Bureau of Education*

PEDRO ROSSELLÓ

The failure of the League to make education its active concern led in 1925 to the establishment of the International Bureau as a private organization. Among its earliest supporters were educators who found their interests not considered by the Committee for Intellectual Cooperation. The early activities of the Bureau are described here, and its Constitution, signed after reorganization in 1929, is reproduced.

THE INTERNATIONAL BUREAU OF EDUCATION AT GENEVA

In the belief that an institution of the kind planned by some of the pioneers would demonstrate the usefulness of an international clearinghouse for educational information, even if it should have to begin on quite a small scale, the International Bureau of Education was founded as a private undertaking in December 1925, at Geneva, by an organising committee backed by the University Institute of Educational Sciences (Jean-Jacques Rousseau Institute). Many eminent educationists and notable international figures took a great interest in its first steps, among them being the Director of the International Labour Office, Albert Thomas. The moving spirit of the organising committee was Professor Edouard Claparède, the distinguished Geneva psychologist.

Within three years, the work accomplished by the staff had abundantly justified the existence of the Bureau, but at the same time it had shown that the means at

* Pedro Rosselló, *Forerunners of the International Bureau of Education,* translated by Marie Butts (London, Evans Brothers, Ltd., 1944), pp. 114-118.

their disposal, furnished by the annual contributions of individual and corporate members, were inadequate for coping with the immense possibilities of international co-operation in the field of education. It was therefore decided to reorganise the Bureau and the new constitution was signed on the 25th of July, 1929. The International Bureau of Education thereby became an official institution controlled, through its Council and Executive Committee, by its members—most of them being Governments or Ministries of Education—who undertook to support it financially. From the outset, Switzerland took the greatest interest in the reorganised institution and gradually a number of other countries joined it; by 1938 it had seventeen members.

The Bureau aims at being a technical and scientific organisation at the service of Ministries of Public Instruction, educational authorities and educationists generally. Its activities are very varied.

It has done a great deal of *research work in comparative education,* through world-wide enquiries carried out by means of questionnaires sent to all Ministries of Education. The findings were published in volumes containing summaries of all the replies received (usually from some fifty governments), along with a general report which was discussed by the *International Conference on Public Instruction,* held every summer, from 1932 to 1939, at Geneva. On the basis of these reports recommendations were adopted by the Conference and sent to Ministries of Public Instruction throughout the world. The invitations to the Conference were sent out by the Swiss Diplomatic Service and it was attended by the official delegates of forty to fifty governments, and by observers from the League of Nations, the International Labour Office and the International Committee on Intellectual Co-operation.

The *publications* of the Bureau number eighty books or pamphlets comprising, besides the above-mentioned reports (on such subjects as: the raising of the school-leaving age, the internal organisation of Ministries of

Education, group-work in the class-room, the professional training of elementary and secondary school teachers, the place of psychology in the formation of teachers, school inspection, the organisation and utilisation of school libraries, the salaries of elementary and secondary school teachers, legislation on school buildings, the drafting, selection and utilisation of school text-books, etc.), national monographs dealing with the educational problems of a given country, and monographs on children's literature.

Since 1931, the Ministries of Public Instruction have been asked for yearly reports on education in their respective countries. These appear, together with school statistics, in the Bureau's educational *Year Book,* issued in French. The edition for 1938 contained official reports from sixty countries; that for 1939, the last one issued, is somewhat smaller.

The International Bureau of Education still publishes a *quarterly Bulletin* (with French and English editions), containing interesting educational items from all over the world and reviews of educational works in several languages. To facilitate the classing in a card-index of the educational news and book reviews, each item is prefixed with its decimal classification number and a subject heading. This *bibilographical service* has proved of great value to educationists.

Until 1940, the Bureau sent out regularly to the leading educational journals of all countries *press-releases* in French and English, thus giving considerable publicity to noteworthy educational innovations, in small as well as great countries of all the continents.

In order that its *information service* may be carried out as efficiently as possible, the Bureau continually adds to its *library* of scientific and practical educational works, school legislation, books on child psychology, educational periodicals (before the war about five hundred periodicals, in many different languages, were received regularly), to its card-index of educational information and to its selected bibliographies, in English and French, on particularly important subjects.

The library of the International Bureau of Education comprises a *Children's Literature Section* containing a large number of children's picture and story books from over forty countries, carefully chosen as being suitable for interesting children in the life of the children of other countries, thus promoting mutual understanding. This section is frequently consulted by librarians, translators, illustrators, parents and teachers. The Bureau has also assembled a fine collection of modern works on history, geography, national and world citizenship, international relations, the revision of history text-books, etc. There are reference books for teachers and for school libraries, as well as text-books and reading books for children of all ages.

The Bureau took the opportunity of its transfer to the Palais Wilson—the building formerly occupied by the Secretariat of the League of Nations—to set up a *Permanent Exhibition of Public Instruction,* where all the governments effectively contributing to its financing have at their disposal a section, to be used for the purpose of acquainting other nations with the system and methods of education in their own land. Amongst others, the outstanding exhibits of Switzerland and Poland have attracted much attention.

The International Bureau of Education has corresponded with education authorities, teachers of all categories, parents and students from every part of the world: between the 1st of July, 1940 and the 30th of June, 1941, although hampered by difficulties in correspondence entailed by the war, it received 10,134 letters and despatched 17,217. It was frequently able to establish mutually helpful contacts between educationists of different and often widely separated countries, who faced the same problems or were interested in the same subjects, and to give to such as desired it information or advice in respect to the educational systems, methods or institutions they would find it most useful to study carefully, if possible at first hand. The Bureau also benefited by the fact that Geneva— owing to the presence within its walls of the headquarters of the League of Nations, the International Labour Office and many of the most important of the unofficial international organisations—was a world centre: it was privileged to receive the visit of many distinguished educationists, as well as of countless enquirers, from every conceivable country in all the continents.

CONSTITUTION OF THE INTERNATIONAL BUREAU OF EDUCATION (GENEVA, 1929)

Preamble.—Being convinced that the development of education is an essential factor in the establishment of peace and in the moral and material progress of humanity,

That, with a view to promoting this development, it is important to collect educational data through investigation and research, and to facilitate the exchange of such information for the purpose of encouraging each country to profit by the experience of others,

Article 1.—An institution of universal interest, to be known as the "International Bureau of Education," is hereby created.

Article 2.—The object of the International Bureau of Education is to act as an information centre for all matters relating to education.

The Bureau, which aims to promote international co-operation, maintains a completely neutral position with regard to national, political and religious questions. As an organ of information and investigation, its work is carried on in a strictly scientific and objective spirit. Its activities are of two kinds: (1) the collection of information relating to public and private education; (2) the initiation of scientific investigations within its sphere and the undertaking of statistical enquiries or those relating to experimental projects. The results of these efforts are made available to educators.

Article 3.—The seat of the International Bureau of Education is at Geneva.

Article 4.—The above-mentioned bodies* are recognised as members of the International Bureau of Education; and, subject to the approval of the Council, a Government, a public institution or an international organisation, paying a minimum annual contribution of 10,000 Swiss francs, may become members of the International Bureau of Education.

Article 5.—The rights of membership in the International Bureau of Education are limited to the period for which members have paid their subscriptions.

Article 6.—A member may withdraw from the Bureau by submitting its resignation. This, however, becomes effective only after a year's notice, beginning at the end of the current fiscal year.

Article 7.—The organs of the International Bureau of Education are: the Council, the Executive Committee, Commissions and a Secretarial Staff.

Article 8.—The Council is the controlling power of the International Bureau of Education. It is composed of three representatives from each of the members and meets once a year. A plenary meeting, however, is held whenever a request for the same is made by not less than one-third of the members.

Article 9.—The functions of the Council are:

(*a*) To determine the general policy and to outline the work undertaken by the International Bureau of Education.

(*b*) To hear the report of the Executive Committee and the reports of the Commissions on matters dealt with between Council meetings.

(*c*) To appoint the members of the Executive Committee and of the various Commissions on which there shall

---

* These were the first four signatories of the constitution, i.e. three countries and the University Institute of Educational Sciences, of Geneva.

be an equitable representation of members and of countries.

(*d*) To approve the expenditure and to examine the accounts.

(*e*) To consider amendments to the Constitution and By-Laws.

Article 10.—The Council is duly constituted whatever may be the number of members present at a meeting.

Article 11.—The Council delegates its powers to the Executive Committee, which acts between the sessions of the Council. The Executive Committee meets at the call of the Chairman. It consists of the Chairman, two Vice-Chairmen and as many other members as the Council may decide. The Council elects the Executive Committee every two years. The members of the Executive Committee may be re-elected.

Article 12.—The Council appoints a Standing Advisory Committee, consisting of from fifteen to thirty members, whose function it is to report on questions submitted to it by the Council and to bring to the latter's notice the most pressing needs of the educational world. It also appoints a Financial Committee.

Article 13.—The Council appoints Commissions to deal with special questions, whenever this seems advisable.

Article 14.—At the head of the Bureau, there is a Director, who with the secretarial staff, conducts the technical and administrative work. He is appointed, as others of the personnel, by the Executive Committee.

Article 15.—The resources of the International Bureau of Education consist of: the regular subscriptions of its members; gifts and bequests, subject to acceptance by the Executive Committee; the proceeds from the sale of its publications; donations allocated for special work in the field of its activity, which in each case shall be approved by the Executive Committee.

Article 16.—The Council may, by a two-thirds majority of those present and voting, amend this Constitution at any time, provided the proposals for amendments have been placed on the agenda three months before the Council meeting.

Article 17.—The International Bureau of Education may be dissolved by a two-thirds majority of the Council convened for this special purpose. In case of dissolution, the Council shall transfer the property of the Bureau to such agency or agencies which can most effectively continue the work undertaken by the Bureau.

The present Constitution was adopted on July 25th, 1929.

"Since Wars Begin in the Minds of Men . . ."

The approval of a constitution for UNESCO in 1945 represented the culmination of several years of work by the Allied Ministers of Education, meeting "in exile" in England during World War II. However, it also represented the cumulative experience of all the preceding international organizations and pioneers in international education. For the first time, "education" was considered to be a major function of an intergovernmental organization representing the majority of countries of the world.

CONSTITUTION OF THE UNITED NATIONS EDUCATIONAL, SCIENTIFIC AND CULTURAL ORGANISATION *

London, 16th November, 1945

THE Governments of the States parties to this Constitution on behalf of their peoples declare, that since wars begin in the minds of men, it is in the minds of men that the defences of peace must be constructed;

that ignorance of each other's ways and lives has been a common cause, throughout the history of mankind, of that suspicion and mistrust between the peoples of the world through which their differences have all too often broken into war;

that the great and terrible war which has now ended was a war made possible by the denial of the democratic

* *Conference for the Establishment of the United Nations Educational, Scientific and Cultural Organisation* (London, UNESCO, 1946), pp. 93-99.

principles of the dignity, equality and mutual respect of men, and by the propagation, in their place, through ignorance and prejudice, of the doctrine of the inequality of men and races;

that the wide diffusion of culture, and the education of humanity for justice and liberty and peace are indispensable to the dignity of man and constitute a sacred duty which all the nations must fulfil in a spirit of mutual assistance and concern;

that a peace based exclusively upon the political and economic arrangements of governments would not be a peace which could secure the unanimous lasting and sincere support of the peoples of the world, and that the peace must therefore be founded, if it is not to fail, upon the intellectual and moral solidarity of mankind.

For these reasons, the States parties to this Constitution, believing in full and equal opportunities for education for all, in the unrestricted pursuit of objective truth, and in the free exchange of ideas and knowledge, are agreed and determined to develop and to increase the means of communication between their peoples and to employ these means for the purposes of mutual understanding and a truer and more perfect knowledge of each other's lives;

In consequence whereof they do hereby create the United Nations Educational, Scientific and Cultural Organisation for the purpose of advancing, through the educational and scientific and cultural relations of the peoples of the world, the objectives of international peace and of the common welfare of mankind for which the United Nations Organisation was established and which its Charter proclaims.

ARTICLE I

PURPOSES AND FUNCTIONS

1. The purpose of the Organisation is to contribute to peace and security by promoting collaboration among the nations through education, science and culture in order to further universal respect for justice, for the rule

of law and for the human rights and fundamental freedoms which are affirmed for the peoples of the world, without distinction of race, sex, language or religion, by the Charter of the United Nations.

2. To realise this purpose the Organisation will:

(*a*) collaborate in the work of advancing the mutual knowledge and understanding of peoples, through all means of mass communication and to that end recommend such international agreements as may be necessary to promote the free flow of ideas by word and image;

(*b*) give fresh impulse to popular education and to the spread of culture:

by collaborating with Members, at their request, in the development of educational activities;
by instituting collaboration among the nations to advance the ideal of equality of educational opportunity without regard to race, sex or any distinctions, economic or social;
by suggesting educational methods best suited to prepare the children of the world for the responsibilities of freedom;

(*c*) maintain, increase and diffuse knowledge:

by assuring the conservation and protection of the world's inheritance of books, works of art and monuments of history and science, and recommending to the nations concerned the necessary international conventions;
by encouraging co-operation among the nations in all branches of intellectual activity, including the international exchange of persons active in the fields of education, science and culture and the exchange of publications, objects of artistic and scientific interest and other materials of information;
by initiating methods of international co-opera-

tion calculated to give the people of all countries access to the printed and published materials produced by any of them.

3. With a view to preserving the independence, integrity and fruitful diversity of the cultures and educational systems of the States Members of this Organisation, the Organisation is prohibited from intervening in matters which are essentially within their domestic jurisdiction.

ARTICLE II

MEMBERSHIP

1. Membership of the United Nations Organisation shall carry with it the right to membership of the United Nations Educational, Scientific and Cultural Organisation.

2. Subject to the conditions of the agreement between this Organisation and the United Nations Organisation, approved pursuant to Article X of this Constitution, States not members of the United Nations Organisation may be admitted to membership of the Organisation, upon recommendation of the Executive Board, by a two-thirds majority vote of the General Conference.

3. Members of the Organisation which are suspended from the exercise of the rights and privileges of membership of the United Nations Organisation shall, upon the request of the latter, be suspended from the rights and privileges of this Organisation.

4. Members of the Organisation which are expelled from the United Nations Organisation shall automatically cease to be members of this Organisation.

ARTICLE III

ORGANS

The Organisation shall include a General Conference, an Executive Board and a Secretariat.

ARTICLE IV

The General Conference

A.—*Composition.*

1. The General Conference shall consist of the representatives of the States Members of the Organisation. The Government of each Member State shall appoint not more than five delegates, who shall be selected after consultation with the National Commission, if established, or with educational, scientific and cultural bodies.

B.—*Functions.*

2. The General Conference shall determine the policies and the main lines of work of the Organisation. It shall take decisions on programmes drawn up by the Executive Board.

3. The General Conference shall, when it deems it desirable, summon international conferences on education, the sciences and humanities and the dissemination of knowledge.

4. The General Conference shall, in adopting proposals for submission to the Member States, distinguish between recommendations and international conventions submitted for their approval. In the former case a majority vote shall suffice; in the latter case a two-thirds majority shall be required. Each of the Member States shall submit recommendations or conventions to its competent authorities within a period of one year from the close of the session of the General Conference at which they were adopted.

5. The General Conference shall advise the United Nations Organisation on the educational, scientific and cultural aspects of matters of concern to the latter, in accordance with the terms and procedure agreed upon between the appropriate authorities of the two Organisations.

6. The General Conference shall receive and consider the reports submitted periodically by Member States as provided by Article VIII.

7. The General Conference shall elect the members of

the Executive Board and, on the recommendation of the Board, shall appoint the Director-General.

C.—*Voting*.

8. Each Member State shall have one vote in the General Conference. Decisions shall be made by a simple majority except in cases in which a two-thirds majority is required by the provisions of this Constitution. A majority shall be a majority of the Members present and voting.

D.—*Procedure*.

9. The General Conference shall meet annually in ordinary session: it may meet in extraordinary session on the call of the Executive Board. At each session the location of its next session shall be designated by the General Conference and shall vary from year to year.

10. The General Conference shall, at each session, elect a President and other officers and adopt rules of procedure.

11. The General Conference shall set up special and technical committees and such other subordinate bodies as may be necessary for its purposes.

12. The General Conference shall cause arrangements to be made for public access to meetings, subject to such regulations as it shall prescribe.

E.—*Observers*.

13. The General Conference, on the recommendation of the Executive Board and by a two-thirds majority, may, subject to its rules of procedure, invite as observers at specified sessions of the Conference or of its commissions representatives of international organisations, such as those referred to in Article XI, paragraph 4.

ARTICLE V

EXECUTIVE BOARD

A.—*Composition*.

1. The Executive Board shall consist of eighteen members elected by the General Conference from among the

delegates appointed by the Member States, together with the President of the Conference who shall sit *ex officio* in an advisory capacity.

2. In electing the members of the Executive Board the General Conference shall endeavour to include persons competent in the arts, the humanities, the sciences, education and the diffusion of ideas, and qualified by their experience and capacity to fulfil the administrative and executive duties of the Board. It shall also have regard to the diversity of cultures and a balanced geographical distribution. Not more than one national of any Member State shall serve on the Board at any one time, the President of the Conference excepted.

3. The elected members of the Executive Board shall serve for a term of three years, and shall be immediately eligible for a second term, but shall not serve consecutively for more than two terms. At the first election eighteen members shall be elected of whom one-third shall retire at the end of the first year and one-third at the end of the second year, the order of retirement being determined immediately after the election by the drawing of lots. Thereafter six members shall be elected each year.

4. In the event of the death or resignation of one of its members, the Executive Board shall appoint, from among the delegates of the Member State concerned, a substitute, who shall serve until the next session of the General Conference which shall elect a member for the remainder of the term.

B.—*Functions.*

5. The Executive Board, acting under the authority of the General Conference, shall be responsible for the execution of the programme adopted by the Conference and shall prepare its agenda and programme of work.

6. The Executive Board shall recommend to the General Conference the admission of new Members to the Organisation.

7. Subject to decisions of the General Conference, the Executive Board shall adopt its own rules of procedure. It shall elect its officers from among its members.

8. The Executive Board shall meet in regular session at least twice a year and may meet in special session if convoked by the Chairman on his own initiative or upon the request of six members of the Board.

9. The Chairman of the Executive Board shall present to the General Conference, with or without comment, the annual report of the Director-General on the activities of the Organisation, which shall have been previously submitted to the Board.

10. The Executive Board shall make all necessary arrangements to consult the representatives of international organisations or qualified persons concerned with questions within its competence.

11. The members of the Executive Board shall exercise the powers delegated to them by the General Conference on behalf of the Conference as a whole and not as representatives of their respective Governments.

ARTICLE VI

SECRETARIAT

1. The Secretariat shall consist of a Director-General and such staff as may be required.

2. The Director-General shall be nominated by the Executive Board and appointed by the General Conference for a period of six years, under such conditions as the Conference may approve, and shall be eligible for reappointment. He shall be the chief administrative officer of the Organisation.

3. The Director-General, or a deputy designated by him, shall participate, without the right to vote, in all meetings of the General Conference, of the Executive Board, and of the committees of the Organisation. He shall formulate proposals for appropriate action by the Conference and the Board.

4. The Director-General shall appoint the staff of the Secretariat in accordance with staff regulations to be approved by the General Conference. Subject to the paramount consideration of securing the highest standards of integrity, efficiency and technical competence, ap-

pointment to the staff shall be on as wide a geographical basis as possible.

5. The responsibilities of the Director-General and of the staff shall be exclusively international in character. In the discharge of their duties they shall not seek or receive instructions from any Government or from any authority external to the Organisation. They shall refrain from any action which might prejudice their position as international officials. Each State Member of the Organisation undertakes to respect the international character of the responsibilities of the Director-General and the staff, and not to seek to influence them in the discharge of their duties.

6. Nothing in this Article shall preclude the Organisation from entering into special arrangements within the United Nations Organisation for common services and staff and for the interchange of personnel.

ARTICLE VII

NATIONAL CO-OPERATING BODIES

1. Each Member State shall make such arrangements as suit its particular conditions for the purpose of associating its principal bodies interested in educational, scientific and cultural matters with the work of the Organisation, preferably by the formation of a National Commission broadly representative of the Government and such bodies.

2. National Commissions or national co-operating bodies, where they exist, shall act in an advisory capacity to their respective delegations to the General Conference and to their Governments in matters relating to the Organisation and shall function as agencies of liaison in all matters of interest to it.

3. The Organisation may, on the request of a Member State, delegate, either temporarily or permanently, a member of its Secretariat to serve on the National Commission of that State, in order to assist in the development of its work.

ARTICLE VIII

REPORTS BY MEMBER STATES

Each Member State shall report periodically to the Organisation, in a manner to be determined by the General Conference, on its laws, regulations and statistics relating to educational, scientific and cultural life and institutions, and on the action taken upon the recommendations and conventions referred to in Article IV, paragraph 4.

ARTICLE IX

BUDGET

1. The Budget shall be administered by the Organisation.

2. The General Conference shall approve and give final effect to the budget and to the apportionment of financial responsibility among the States Members of the Organisation subject to such arrangement with the United Nations as may be provided in the agreement to be entered into pursuant to Article X.

3. The Director-General, with the approval of the Executive Board, may receive gifts, bequests, and subventions directly from Governments, public and private institutions, associations and private persons.

ARTICLE X

RELATIONS WITH THE UNITED NATIONS ORGANISATION

This Organisation shall be brought into relation with the United Nations Organisation, as soon as practicable, as one of the specialised agencies referred to in Article 57 of the Charter of the United Nations. This relationship shall be effected through an agreement with the United Nations Organisation under Article 63 of the Charter, which agreement shall be subject to the approval of the General Conference of this Organisation. The agreement shall provide for effective co-operation between the two Organisations in the pursuit of their common purposes, and at the same time shall recognise the autonomy of this Organisation, within the fields of its competence as defined in this Constitution. Such agreement may, among other matters, provide for the approval and financing of the budget of the Organisation by the General Assembly of the United Nations.

ARTICLE XI

Relations with other specialised international Organisations and agencies

1. This Organisation may co-operate with other specialised inter-governmental organisations and agencies whose interests and activities are related to its purposes. To this end the Director-General, acting under the general authority of the Executive Board, may establish effective working relationships with such organisations and agencies and establish such joint committees as may be necessary to assure effective co-operation. Any formal arrangements entered into with such organisations or agencies shall be subject to the approval of the Executive Board.

2. Whenever the General Conference of this Organisation and the competent authorities of any other specialised inter-governmental organisations or agencies whose purposes and functions lie within the competence of this Organisation, deem it desirable to effect a transfer of their resources and activities to this Organisation, the Director-General, subject to the approval of the Conference, may enter into mutually acceptable arrangements for this purpose.

3. This Organisation may make appropriate arrangements with other inter-governmental organisations for reciprocal representation at meetings.

4. The United Nations Educational, Scientific and Cultural Organisation may make suitable arrangements for consultation and co-operation with non-governmental international organisations concerned with matters within its competence, and may invite them to undertake specific tasks. Such co-operation may also include

appropriate participation by representatives of such organisations on advisory committees set up by the General Conference.

ARTICLE XII

LEGAL STATUS OF THE ORGANISATION

The provisions of Articles 104 and 105 of the Charter of the United Nations Organisation concerning the legal status of that Organisation, its privileges and immunities shall apply in the same way to this Organisation.

ARTICLE XIII

AMENDMENTS

1. Proposals for amendments to this Constitution shall become effective upon receiving the approval of the General Conference by a two-thirds majority; provided, however, that those amendments which involve fundamental alterations in the aims of the Organisation or new obligations for the Member States shall require subsequent acceptance on the part of two-thirds of the Member States before they come into force. The draft texts of proposed amendments shall be communicated by the Director-General to the Member States at least six months in advance of their consideration by the General Conference.

2. The General Conference shall have power to adopt by a two-thirds majority rules of procedure for carrying out the provisions of this Article.

ARTICLE XIV

INTERPRETATION

1. The English and French texts of this Constitution shall be regarded as equally authoritative.

2. Any question or dispute concerning the interpretation of this Constitution shall be referred for determination to the International Court of Justice or to an arbitral tribunal, as the General Conference may determine under its rules of procedure.

ARTICLE XV

ENTRY INTO FORCE

1. This Constitution shall be subject to acceptance. The instruments of acceptance shall be deposited with the Government of the United Kingdom.

2. This Constitution shall remain open for signature in the archives of the Government of the United Kingdom. Signature may take place either before or after the deposit of the instrument of acceptance. No acceptance shall be valid unless preceded or followed by signature.

3. This Constitution shall come into force when it has been accepted by twenty of its signatories. Subsequent acceptances shall take effect immediately.

4. The Government of the United Kingdom will inform all members of the United Nations of the receipt of all instruments of acceptance and of the date on which the Constitution comes into force in accordance with the preceding paragraph.

In faith whereof, the undersigned, duly authorised to that effect, have signed this Constitution in the English and French languages, both texts being equally authentic.

Done in London the sixteenth day of November, 1945, in a single copy, in the English and French languages, of which certified copies will be communicated by the Government of the United Kingdom to the Governments of all the Members of the United Nations.

INSTRUMENT ESTABLISHING A PREPARATORY EDUCATIONAL, SCIENTIFC AND CULTURAL COMMISSION

London, 16th November, 1945

THE Governments represented at the United Nations Educational and Cultural Conference in London,

Having determined that an international organisation to be known as the United Nations Educational, Scientific and Cultural Organisation shall be established, and

Having formulated the Constitution of the United

Nations Educational, Scientific and Cultural Organisation,

Agree as follows:—

1. Pending the coming into force of the Constitution and the establishment of the Organisation provided for therein, there shall be established a Preparatory Commission to make arrangements for the first Session of the General Conference of the Organisation, and to take such other steps as are indicated below.

2. For this purpose the Commission shall:—

(a) Convoke the First Session of the General Conference.

(b) Prepare the provisional agenda for the First Session of the General Conference and prepare documents and recommendations relating to all matters on the agenda including such matters as the possible transfer of functions, activities and assets of existing international agencies, the specific arrangements between this Organisation and the United Nations Organisation, and arrangements for the Secretariat of the Organisation and the appointment of its Director-General.

(c) Make studies and prepare recommendations concerning the programme and the budget of the Organisation for presentation to the General Conference at its First Session.

(d) Provide without delay for immediate action on urgent needs of educational, scientific, and cultural reconstruction in devastated countries as indicated in Paragraphs 6 and 7.

3. The Commission shall consist of one representative of each of the Governments signatory to this Instrument.

4. The Commission shall appoint an Executive Committee composed of fifteen members to be selected at the first meeting of the Commission. The Executive Committee shall exercise any or all powers of the Commission as the Commission may determine.

5. The Commission shall establish its own rules of procedure and shall appoint such other committees and

consult with such specialists as may be desirable to facilitate its work.

6. The Commission shall appoint a special technical sub-committee to examine the problems relating to the educational, scientific and cultural needs of the countries devastated by the war, having regard to the information already collected and the work being done by other international organisations, and to prepare as complete a conspectus as possible of the extent and nature of the problems for the information of the Organisation at the First Session of the Conference.

7. When the technical sub-committee is satisfied that any ameliorative measures are immediately practicable to meet any educational, scientific or cultural needs it shall report to the Commission accordingly and the Commission shall, if it approves, take steps to bring such needs to the attention of Governments, organisations, and persons wishing to assist by contributing money, supplies or services in order that co-ordinated relief may be given either directly by the donors to the countries requiring aid or indirectly through existing international relief organisations.

8. The Commission shall appoint an Executive Secretary who shall exercise such powers and perform such duties as the Commission may determine, with such international staff as may be required. The staff shall be composed as far as possible of officials and specialists made available for this purpose by the participating Governments on the invitation of the Executive Secretary.

9. The provisions of Articles 104 and 105 of the Charter of the United Nations Organisation concerning the legal status of that Organisation, its privileges and immunities shall apply in the same way to this Commission.

10. The Commission shall hold its first meeting in London immediately after the conclusion of the present Conference and shall continue to sit in London until such time as the Constitution of the Organisation has come into force. The Commission shall then transfer to Paris where the permanent Organisation is to be located.

11. During such period as the Commission is in London, the expenses of its maintenance shall be met by the Government of the United Kingdom on the understanding:

(1) that the amount of the expenses so incurred will be deducted from the contributions of that Government to the new Organisation until they have been recovered, and

(2) that it will be open to the Commission, if circumstances so warrant, to seek contributions from other Governments.

When the Commission is transferred to Paris, the financial responsibility will pass to the French Government on the same terms.

12. The Commission shall cease to exist upon the assumption of office of the Director-General of the Organisation, at which time its property and records shall be transferred to the Organisation.

13. The Government of the United Kingdom shall be the temporary depositary and shall have custody of the original document embodying these interim arrangements in the English and French languages. The Government of the United Kingdom shall transfer the original to the Director-General on his assumption of office.

14. This Instrument shall be effective as from this date, and shall remain open for signature on behalf of the States entitled to be the original Members of the United Nations Educational, Scientific and Cultural Organisation, until the Commission is dissolved in accordance with paragraph 12.

In faith whereof, the undersigned representatives, having been duly authorised for that purpose, have signed this Instrument in the English and French languages, both texts being equally authentic.

Done in London the Sixteenth day of November, 1945, in a single copy, in the English and French languages, of which certified copies will be communicated by the Government of the United Kingdom to the Governments of all the States Members of the United Nations.

Part III
WHEN PEOPLES MEET

->>)«<-

East–West Understanding*

GILBERT MURRAY~
RABINDRANATH TAGORE

The lack of understanding between Eastern and Western cultures has led UNESCO to encourage the exchange of cultural materials. No better example of the exchange of frank ideas between the two cultures exists than the exchange of letters between Gilbert Murray and Rabindranath Tagore. Murray, one of the leading scholars of the Western world, was instrumental in the establishment of the Committee on Intellectual Cooperation. Tagore, one of the great poets of the present century, devoted his life to the improvement of education in India.

Yatscombe, Boar's Hill, Oxford
August 17th, 1934

My dear Tagore,

I venture to trouble you with this letter for several reasons. First, you are a great poet, probably the most famous poet now living in the world, and poetry is to me almost the chief pleasure and interest in life. Your life and work are inspired by a spirit of harmony, and it is in the interest of harmony between man and man that I make my appeal. You are a Thinker, and in this distracted world, where nation stands armed against nation and the old liberal statesmanship of the nineteenth

* Gilbert Murray and Rabindranath Tagore, *East and West: An International Series of Open Letters* (Paris: International Institute of Intellectual Cooperation, 1935).

century seems to have given way to a blind temper of competition, I cannot but look to the Thinkers of the world to stand together, not in one nation but in all nations, reminding all who care to listen of the reality of human brotherhood and the impossibility of basing a durable civilized society on any foundation save peace and the will to act justly.

All generalizations about whole nations or groups of nations are superficial and inaccurate, even when made by scientific students without personal bias. And most of these actually current are made by prejudiced and utterly unscientific partisans. People talk loosely of the difference in character between "Nordic" and "Latin" nations, or, in still looser phrase, between "East" and "West" violently denouncing the one and praising the other. Even when there is no actual prejudice at work, the comparisons, though sometimes suggestive, are never exact. For one thing, neither side of the comparison is uniform: every German is different from every other German, every Italian from every other Italian: nor can you make any single statement that will be true of all Indians or of all Englishmen. And besides, the differences of habits and ways of thought between, say, one fairly typical Bengali and one typical Yorkshireman, are so infinite in number that they cannot be added together in a definite catalogue, and for the most part so utterly unimportant that they would not be worth cataloguing. I am always puzzled by the people who ask me "Do I like Indians" or it may be Americans or Frenchmen; and can only answer, as I would about by own countrymen, that I like some and do not like others.

Yet the differences are there, and are felt though they cannot be analyzed. Indeed the mischief is that they are felt far too much; infinitesimal peculiarities are noted and interpreted as having some great moral significance. We are accustomed to our own people and do not seek for profound psychological explanations of their chance looks and ways. But when we meet a foreigner we feel a surge of curiosity and criticism rising within us. We want eagerly to know what this strange being is really like, and we have so little evidence to go upon that we exaggerate the importance of all we have. A slightly louder voice, a less ceremonious address, a ruddier face, will suggest insolence and brutality: the opposite will seem to be symptoms of timidity and insincerity. Similarly, an act of courtesy to which we are not accustomed will be gratefully remembered for years; a breach of the sort of courtesy which we expect will be furiously resented. And, inevitably when this course of ingenious misinterpretation is once begun, it is easy to get abundant confirmation of all one's prejudices. It is said to be, in point of law, impossible to draw an indictment against a nation: as a matter of literature, it is only too easy. One could write a "Mother India" about every nation—an appalling indictment, and false as a whole, while every statement in it might be true. I remember an English newspaper in the 90's which, finding nothing more mischievous to do at the moment, used to collect and publish a list of all the crimes committed by members of the French army. And since the French army was very large the crimes were proportionately numerous, and the effect as horrifying as the editor desired. Many of us read a famous German scholar's book, "England" published during the war. It dwelt upon the disgusting faults of the English and the merits of the writer's own countrymen, and perhaps, in the long run, it was as useful to us as it was harmful to them. But of course the whole method of such books is wrong. The first step towards international understanding must be a recognition that our own national habits are not the unfailing canon by which those of other peoples must be judged, and that the beginning of all improvement must be a certain reasonable humility.

It is not hard, in theory at least, to make this first step. Indeed it is a duty generally recognized by English Liberals. The historical works of my friend, Edward Thompson, on Indian subjects are an example. But it is hard indeed to carry out consistently, and even to begin needs some imaginative effort.

An Indian friend of mine once told me that as a small

child he had been taught to regard the Englishman as something scarcely human, a kind of Demon, which had every day both to shed blood and be drugged with alcohol, or else its rage became terrible. This, I suppose, was strictly true, at any rate of some average British officers on a hunting expedition. They did expect every day to shed blood and to cheer themselves with alcohol—two acts which to my Indian friend were equally abominable; and I can quite believe that their tempers wore rather thin when they were disappointed of either. Yet no doubt, apart from this little weakness for blood and alcohol, they were excellent people.

I remember many years ago a visit of yours to England, when a number of people met to give you a public welcome in some hall in London, and, among other features in the entertainment, an English singer sang one of your poems. It was a gentle philosophical poem, dependent for its whole effect upon a spirit of quiet and calm. I should have liked to hear it spoken to the accompaniment of some antique stringed instrument like a harp or a cithara. But on this occasion it had been set to modern European music of a bravura style, and when the singer began, her piercing soprano made me wince. I looked to see how you were bearing it. No doubt you suffered, but you were the centre of all eyes and your statuesque courtesy was undisturbed.

Yes, the differences are there: they are real and perhaps to a certain extent they are national or racial, though not so much as people imagine. I was once on a Committee where a certain Indian member was making himself very tiresome (there are tiresome Indians as well as tiresome Europeans) by his touchiness and vanity. And a wise old Japanese friend of mine told me afterwards how he had wondered within himself: "Is that sort of behaviour Asiatic, and ought I to feel ashamed? Or is it Indo-European, so that I am left untouched?" Of course it was neither. It was only human. There are touchy and vain people in all parts of the world, just as there are criminals in all parts; just as there are thinkers, artists, poets, men of learning; just as there are saints and sages.

And it is valuable to remember that, as Plato pointed out long ago, while criminals tend to cheat and fight one another, and stupid people to misunderstand one another, there is a certain germ of mutual sympathy between people of good will or good intelligence. An artist cannot help liking good art, a poet good poetry, a man of science good scientific work, from whatever country it may spring. And that common love of beauty or truth, a spirit indifferent to races and frontiers, ought, among all the political discords and antagonisms of the world, to be a steady well-spring of good understanding, a permanent agency of union and brotherhood.

There is no need for sentimentality, no need for pretence. If I enjoy the beauty of your poetry, if I sympathize with your rejection of honours from a government which you had ceased to respect, that makes already a sufficient bond between us: there is no need for me to share, or pretend to share, or make a great effort to share, your views on every subject, or because I admire certain things that are Indian to turn round and denounce Western Civilization. Men of imagination appreciate what is different from themselves: that is the great power which imagination gives. For example, I have just been reading your play called in French "La Machine" and see in it, if I am not mistaken, your hatred of machines as such, and of all the mechanization of modern life. Now I happen to admire machines and the engineers who make them. I respect their educational influence. I feel that if a boy's horse or dog will not do what he wants he will probably try to make it do so by losing his temper and beating it; but if his bicycle or his wireless will not work, he knows it is no good losing his temper. He has to think and work, to find out what is wrong and to put it right: which is a priceless lesson for any boy. Then the use of machinery teaches conscientiousness to the mechanic. I often think of the thousands and thousands of aeroplanes that are plying their daily tasks throughout Europe and America; each one of them consisting of thousands and thousands of parts, every single one of which must be properly adjusted and made fast by the workmen before the machine starts. A mistake, almost any mistake, is quite likely to be fatal. But the engineers, quite ordinary men for the most part, are so trained that they do not make a mistake, and the rest of us have such confidence in their accuracy and conscientiousness that we travel in their aeroplanes freely and without a qualm. This seems to me a quite wonderful fact, that masses of men should have been made so trustworthy and reliable. It is the Age of Machines that, for the first time in history, has made them so. I write this not to argue but merely to illustrate; to show that difference of opinion, habit or training need not cause alienation. You can remain profoundly Indian and I a regular westerner, without disturbance to our mutual sympathy.

I even believe in the healthiness and high moral quality of our poor distressed civilization. It made the most ghastly war in history, but it hated itself for doing so. As a result of the war it is now full of oppressions, cruelties, stupidities and public delusions of a kind which were thought to be obsolete and for ever discarded a century ago. But I doubt if ever before there was what theologians would call such a general sense of sin, such widespread consciousness of the folly and wickedness in which most nations and governments are involved, or such a determined effort, in spite of failure after failure, to get rid at last of war and the fear of war and all the baseness and savagery which that fear engenders. I still have hope for the future of this tortured and criminal generation: perhaps you have lost hope and perhaps you will prove right. But the divergence of view need make no rift between us.

My beloved and admired colleague, Mme Curie, when she threw herself into the work of Intellectual Co-operation, gave one special reason for doing so. She had seen, during the World War, how often the intellectual leaders in the various nations had been not better but, if anything, worse than the common people in the bitterness and injustice of their feelings. She had seen that this was a great evil and one that could be remedied. The artists and thinkers, the people whose work or whose words move multitudes, ought to know one another, to understand one another, to work together at the formation of some great League of Mind or Thought independent of miserable frontiers and tariffs and governmental follies, a League or Society of those who live the life of the intellect and through the diverse channels of art or science aim at the attainment of beauty, truth and human brotherhood.

I need not appeal to you, Tagore, to join in this quest; you already belong to it; you are inevitably one of its great leaders. I only ask you to recognize the greatness of your own work for the intellectual union of East and West, of thinker with thinker and poet with poet, and to appreciate the work that may be done by the intellectuals of India not merely for their own national aims, however just and reasonable they may be; there is a higher task to be attempted in healing the discords of the political and material world by the magic of that inward community of spiritual life which even amid our worst failures reveals to us Children of Men our brotherhood and our high destiny.

Believe me, with deep respect,

Yours sincerely,

GILBERT MURRAY

"Uttarayan" Santiniketan, Bengal
September 16th, 1934

My dear Professor Murray.

In the midst of my busy seclusion in a corner of this Educational Colony in India comes your letter bearing its call for close understanding of the problems that face our common humanity. I have no difficulty in responding to your friendly voice, for it is not only the voice of a friend whom I have the privilege to know and love; but it also carries the highest authority of European culture and scholarship, and is therefore eminently fitted to represent the great humanity of Europe.

I must confess at once that I do not see any solution of the intricate evils of disharmonious relationship between nations, nor can I point out any path which may lead us immediately to the levels of sanity. Like yourself, I find much that is deeply distressing in modern conditions, and I am in complete agreement with you again in believing that at no other period of history has mankind as a whole been more alive to the need of human co-operation, more conscious of the inevitable and inescapable moral links which hold together the fabric of human civilization. I cannot afford to lose my faith in this inner spirit of Man, nor in the sureness of human progress which following the upward path of struggle and travail is constantly achieving, through cyclic darkness and doubt, its ever-widening ranges of fulfilment. Willingly therefore I harness myself, in my advanced age, to the arduous responsibility of creating in our Educational Colony in Santiniketan a spirit of genuine international collaboration based on a definite pursuit of knowledge, a pursuit carried on in an atmosphere of friendly community life, harmonized with Nature, and offering freedom of individual self-expression. This work which I have to continue in the face of desperately adverse circumstance, has yet struck root in the soil of India, and sent out its branches to a wider arena of humanity, and it carries, I believe, a very deep affinity with the activities with which I am already associated.

My occasional misgivings about the modern pursuit of Science is directed not against Science, for Science itself can be neither good or evil, but its wrong use. If I may just touch here on your reference to machines, I would say that machines should not be allowed to mechanize human life but contribute to its well being, which as you rightly point out, it is constantly doing when it is man's sanity which controls the use of machinery.

I would like here to quote a passage from one of my writings published in April 1929 which I think may interest you. You will find that it is impossible for me not to accept the true spirit of Science as a pure expression of the creative soul of man.

"Personally I do not believe that Europe is occupied only with material things. She may have lost her faith in religion, but not in humanity. Man, in his essential nature, is spiritual and can never remain solely material. If, however, we in the East merely realize Europe in this external aspect, we shall be seriously at fault. For in Europe the ideals of human activity are truly of the soul. They are not paralyzed by shackles of scriptural injunctions. Their sanction lies in the heart of man and not in something external to him.

"It is this attitude of mind in Europe which is essentially spiritual. . . .

"When the aeroplane goes up in the sky, we may wonder at it as the perfection of material power; but behind this lies the human spirit, strong and alive. It is this spirit of man which has refused to recognize the boundaries of nature as final. Nature has put the fear of death in man's mind to moderate his power within the limits of safety; but man in Europe has snapped his fingers at Death and torn asunder the bonds. Only then did he earn the right to fly—a right of the gods.

"But even here the adverse forces—the Titans—are alive, who are ready to rain down death from the air. But the Titans are not in sole possession. In Europe, there is a constant war between the gods and the Titans. Often the Titans are victorious; but the victory is sometimes with the gods. . . ."

What really must concern us in our generalization or in our detailed study of truth is, as you indicate, a sincere recognition of reality and an unflinching loyalty to it.

May I therefore, in trying to pursue the middle path of harmony, deal with some details of our present problems of India, and also put them in relation to the larger aspect of international relationship as I view it. In offering you gleanings from my thoughts covering a number of my mature years of experience, I may perhaps help in clearing up, to a certain extent, the nature of some of our vital problems. On the clear recognition of these internal as well as international problems must depend the possibility of genuine understanding and co-operation both between the different communities of India and between India as a whole and Europe. This, I believe, is

also the guiding principle of the League of Nations which
has asserted itself time and again in spite of the pressure
of political vicissitudes.

II. Now that mutual intercourse has become easy, and
the different peoples and nations of the world have come
to know one another in various relations, one might have
thought that the time had arrived to merge their differences in a common unity. But the significant thing is,
that the more the doors are opening and the walls break-
ing down outwardly, the greater is the force which the
consciousness of individual distinction is gaining within.
There was a time when we believed that men were re-
maining separate, because of the obstacles between them;
but the removal of these, to the largest possible extent,
is not seen to have the effect of doing away with the differences between diverse sections of mankind.

Individuality is precious, because only through it we
can realize the universal. Unfortunately there are people
who take enormous pride in magnifiying their speciality
and proclaiming to the world that they are fixed for
ever on their pedestal of uniqueness. They forget that
only discords are unique and therefore can claim their
own separate place outside the universal world of music.

It should be the function of religion to provide us
with this universal ideal of truth and maintain it in its
purity. But men have often made perverse use of their
religion, building with it permanent walls to ensure
their own separateness. Christianity, when it minimises
its spiritual truth, which is universal, and emphasizes its
dogmatic side, which is a mere accretion of time, has the
same effect of creating a mental obstruction which leads
to the misunderstanding of people who are outside its
pale. A great deal of the unmerited contempt and cruelty,
which the non-western peoples have suffered in their political, commercial or other relations at the hands of the
West, is owing to sectarian calumnies with which even
the western children's text books are contaminated.
Nevertheless this sectarian religion does not occupy the
greater part of the western life and therefore in its heart

still remains the possibility of a better human relationship than what prevails now between the races.

We have seen Europe cruelly unscrupulous in its politics and commerce, widely spreading slavery over the face of the earth in various names and forms. And yet, in this very same Europe, protest is always alive against its own iniquities. Martyrs are never absent whose lives of sacrifice are the penance for the wrongs done by their own kindred. The individuality which is western is not to be designated by any sect-name of a particular religion, but is distinguished by its eager attitude towards truth, in two of its aspects, scientific and humanistic. This openness of mind to truth has also its moral value and so in the West it has often been noticed that, while those who are professedly pious have sided with tyrannical power, encouraging repression of freedom, the men of intellect, the sceptics, have bravely stood for justice and the rights of man.

I do not mean to say that those who seek truth always find truth, and we know that men in the West are apt to borrow the sanction of science under false pretences to give expression to their passions and prejudices. To many thinkers there has appeared a clear connection between Darwin's theories and the "imperialism" Teutonic and other, which was so marked a feature during the sixties. We have also read western authors who, admirably mimicking scientific mannerism, assert, as you point out, that only the so-called Nordic race has the proper quality and therefore the right to rule the world, extolling its characteristic ruthlessness as giving it the claim to universal dominance. But we must not forget that such aberrations of science, padded with wrong or imperfect data, will be knocked down by science itself. The stream of water in a river does carry sand, but so long as the stream can still flow it will push away the sand from its own path. If the mental attitude is right we need not be afraid of mistakes. That is why the individual in the West has no unsurpassable barrier between himself and the rest of humanity. He may have his prejudices, but no irrational injunctions to keep him in internment away from the wide world of men.

Unfortunately for us, however, the one outstanding visible relationship of Europe with Asia today is that of exploitation; in other words, its origins are commercial and material. It is physical strength that is most apparent to us in Europe's enormous dominion and commerce, illimitable in its extent and immeasurable in its appetite. Our spirit sickens at it. Everywhere we come against barriers in the way of direct human kinship. The harshness of these external contacts is galling, and therefore the feeling of unrest ever grows more oppressive. There is no people in the whole of Asia today which does not look upon Europe with fear and suspicion.

There was a time when we were fascinated by Europe. She had inspired us with a new hope. We believed that her chief mission was to preach the gospel of liberty to the world. We had come then to know only her ideal side through her literature and art. But slowly, Asia and Africa have become the main spheres of Europe's secular activities, where her chief preoccupations have been the earning of dividends, the administration of empires, and the extension of commerce.

Europe's warehouses and business offices, her police outposts and soldiers' barracks, have been multiplied, while her human relationships have declined.

Towards those who are being exploited, there always is wont to grow up a feeling of contempt. For exploitation itself becomes easier, if we can succeed in creating a callousness towards those who are its victims. Just as whenever we go out fishing we are inclined to regard fishes as the least sensitive of all living creatures, so it becomes quite pleasant to loot the Orient, if only we can make our own moral justification easy by relegating coloured races to the lowest groupings of mankind.

Thus modern Europe, scientific and puissant, has portioned out this wide earth into two divisions. Through her filter, whatever is finest in Europe cannot pass through to reach us in the East. In our traffic with her, we have learnt, as the biggest fact of all, that she is efficient, terribly efficient. We may feel astounded by this efficiency; but if, through fear, we bring to it our homage of respect, then we ourselves need to realize that we are fast going down to the very depths of misfortune; for to do such homage is like the crude barbarity of bringing sacrificial offerings to some god which thirsts for blood. It is on account of this fact, and in order to retain her self-respect, that the whole of Asia today denies the moral superiority of Europe. At the same time, to withstand her ravages, Asia is preparing to imitate the ruthless aspect which slays, which eats raw flesh, which tries to make the swallowing process easier by putting the blame on the victim.

But this, as we realize is only one side, however real and painful, of the Western civilization as it appears to us in the East.

Western humanity, when not affected by its unnatural relationship with the East, preserves a singular strength of moral conduct in the domain of its social life, which has its great inspiration for all of us. It is easy enough for us, when someone reviles us for our social evils, to point at worse evils in Europe; but this is negative. The bigger thing to remember is, that in Europe these evils are not stagnant. There, the spiritual force in man is ever trying to come to grips. While, for instance, we find in Europe the evil Giant's fortress of Nationalism, we also find Jack the Giant-Killer. For, there is growing up the international mind. This Giant-Killer, the international mind—though small in size—is real. In India, even when we are loudest in our denunciation of Europe, it is often her Giant's fortress that we long to build with awe and worship. We insult Jack with ridicule and suspicion. The chief reason for this is, that in India we have ourselves become material-minded. We are wanting in faith and courage. Since in our country the gods are sleeping, therefore, when the Titans come, they devour all our sacrificial offerings—there is never a hint of strife. The germs of disease are everywhere; but man can resist disease only when his vital force is active and powerful.

So, too, even when the worship of the blood-thirsty and false gods of self-seeking are rampant on all sides, man can lift up his head to the skies if his spirit is awake. Both matter and spirit are active. They alone become entirely materialistic who are only half men, who cripple the native majesty of the spirit before the blind repetition of unintelligent activities; who are niggardly in knowledge and palsied in action; who are ever insulting themselves by setting up a meaningless ritualism in the place of true worship; who have no difficulty whatever in believing that there is special sanctity inherent in particular forms and peculiar rites, even when their significance is neither known, nor knowable.

I know how reluctant it makes us feel to give any credit for humanity to the western civilization when we observe the brutalities into which this nationalism of theirs breaks out, instances of which are so numerous all the world over—in the late war, in the lynching of negroes, in cowardly outrages allowed to be committed by European soldiers upon helpless Indians, in the rapacity and vandalism practised in Pekin during the Boxer war by the very nations who are never tired of vulgarly applying barbaric epithets to each other according to the vicissitudes of political expediency and passion. But while I have never sought to gloss over or keep out of mind any of these ugly phenomena, I still aver that in the life of the West they have a large tract where their mind is free; whence the circulation of their thought-currents can surround the world. This freedom of the mind's ventilation following the constant growth of a vigorous life bears in it the promise of righting the wrong and purifying the noxious accumulation within.

To me the mere political necessity is unimportant; it is for the sake of our humanity, for the full growth of our soul, that we must turn our mind towards the ideal of the spiritual unity of man. We must use our social strength, not to guard ourselves against the touch of others, considering it as contamination, but generously to extend hospitality to the world, taking all its risks however numerous and grave. We must manfully accept the responsibility of moral freedom, which disdains to barricade itself within dead formulae of external regulation, timidly seeking its security in utter stagnation. Men who live in dread of the spirit of enquiry and lack courage to launch out in the adventure of truth, can never achieve freedom in any department of life. Freedom is not for those who are not lovers of freedom and who only allow it standing space in the porter's vestibule for the sake of some temporary purpose, while worshipping, in the inner shrine of their life, the spirit of blind obedience.

In India what is needed more than anything else, is the broad mind which, only because it is conscious of its own vigorous individuality, is not afraid of accepting truth from all sources. Fortunately for us we know what such a mind has meant in an individual who belongs to modern India. I speak of Rammohun Roy. His learning, because of its depth and comprehensiveness, did not merely furnish him with materials for scholarship, but trained his mind for the free acceptance of truth. Rammohun Roy developed the courage and capacity to discriminate between things that are essential and those that are non-essential in the culture which was his by inheritance. This helped him to realize that truth can never be foreign, that money and material may exclusively belong to the particular country which produces them, but not knowledge, or ideas, or immortal forms of art.

The very magnitude of mind of such men becomes almost a grievance for smaller personalities, and Rammohun has been misunderstood by his own countrymen because he had in him this modern spirit of freedom and comprehensive grasp of truth. We must, however, never make the mistake of thinking that great men who are belittled by their contemporary compatriots do not represent their countries; for countries are not always true to themselves.

In Rammohun Roy's life we find a concrete illustration of what India seeks, the true indication of her goal. Thoroughly steeped in the best culture of his country,

he was capable of finding himself at home in the larger
world. His culture was not for rejection of those cultures
which came from foreign sources; on the contrary, it
had an uncommon power of sympathy which could adjust itself to them with respectful receptiveness.

The ideal I have formed of the culture which should
be universal in India, has become clear to me from the
life of Rammohun Roy. I have come to feel that the
mind which has been matured in the atmosphere of a
profound knowledge of its own country, and of the perfect thoughts that have been produced in that land, is
ready to accept and assimilate the cultures that come
from foreign countries. He who has no wealth of his
own can only beg, and those who are compelled to follow the profession of beggary at the gate of the intellec-
tually rich may gain occasional scraps of mental food, but
they are sure to lose the strength of their intellectual
character and their minds are doomed to become timid
in thought and in creative endeavour.

All this time we have been receiving education on
purely western lines. When this first began, western culture was imbued with a supreme contempt for that of the
East. And to this day, consequently, we have been
brought up in this contempt. This speaks of internal
dissensions within the temple of Mother Saraswati. Her
eastern sons kept closed the door leading to the western
side for fear of adulteration, and her western sons barred
their eastern windows through want of respect. Meanwhile the system of education in India remained, and
still remains, absurdly un-Indian, making no adequate
provision for our own culture. We have, here, not even
anything like the facility which the German student
enjoys in Germany for the study of the lore of Hindu
and Moslem. And if we have become conscious of this
vital deficiency in our education, that is because of the
spirit of the times.

A certain number of us do not admit that our culture
has any special features of value. These good people I
leave out of account. But the number of those others
is not few, who while admitting this value in theory, ig-

nore it more or less in practice. Very often, the flourishing of the banner of this culture is not for the sake of the love of truth but for that of national vain-gloriousness—like brandishing a musical instrument in athletic display before one's own admiring family, instead of using it to make music.

This section of our people while never neglecting to make proud boast of their country's glory, have an absurdly narrow conception of the ideal in which that glory consists. Their indiscriminate reverence is for the actual, not for the eternal. The habits and customs of our decadence which have set up barriers between us and the world, splitting us into mutually exclusive sections, making us weak and bowing our heads in shame at every turn of our later history—these are the idols of their special worship, which they endow with endless virtues of their own imagining. They consider it to be their sacred mission to retain in perpetuity the waste matter sloughed off by age, as the true insignia of our Hindu civilization; to extol the gleam of the will-o'-the-wisp, born of the noxious miasma of decay, as more time-hallowed than the light of sun, moon and stars.

In our greed for immediate political result, we are apt to ascribe the fact of our tendency towards separateness to accidental circumstances, refusing to see that a code of behaviour, which has not the sanction of reason, and yet has the support of religion, must result in the creation of irreconcilable divisions between men. In reason alone can we have our common meeting ground; for that which is against reason needs must be peculiar and exclusive, offering constant friction until worn away by the everactive, rational mind of man. So when, for a body of men, popular custom is artificially protected by a religion which is allowed to usurp the entire range of human knowledge and conduct, it becomes a potent factor in maintaining an immense gap of aloofness and antagonism between closest neighbours.

The evolving Hindu social ideal has never been present to us as a whole, so that we have only a vague conception of what the Hindu has achieved in the past, or can attempt in the future. The partial view, before us at any moment, appears at the time to be the most important, so we can hardly bring ourselves to the true ideal, but tend to destroy it. And there we stand fasting and telling beads, emaciated with doing penance, shrinking into a corner away from the rest of the world.

We forget that Hindu civilization was once very much alive, crossing the seas, planting colonies, giving to and taking from all the world. It had its arts, its commerce, its vast and strenuous field of work. In its history, new ideas had their opportunity. Its women also, had their learning, their bravery, their place in the civic life. In every page of the Mahabharata we shall find proofs that it was no rigid, cast-iron type of civilization. The men of those days did not, like marionettes, play the same set piece over and over again. They progressed through mistakes, made discoveries through experiment, and gained truth through striving. They belonged to a free and varied *Samaj*, quick with life, driven into ever new enterprise by its active vigour.

This, however, was society which orthodoxy today would hardly recognize as Hindu, because it was living and had a growth which was revealing its inner unity through outer changes. So the *dharma* (principle) of life which thinks and doubts, accepts and rejects, progresses, changes and evolves, cannot, according to orthodoxy, be a part of the Hindu Dharma. Man shows his mental feebleness when he loses his faith in life because it is difficult to govern, and is only willing to take the responsibility of the dead because they are content to lie still under an elaborately decorated tomb-stone of his own make. We must know that life carries its own weight, while the burden of the dead is heavy to bear—an intolerable burden which has been pressing upon our country for ages.

The fact stands out clearly today that the Divinity dwelling within the heart of man cannot be kept immured any longer in the darkness of particular temples. The day of the *Ratha-yatra,* the Car Festival, has arrived when He shall come out on the highway of the world, into the thick of the joys and sorrows, the mutual commerce, of the throng of men. Each of us must set to work to build such car as we can, to take its place in the grand procession. The material of some may be of value, of others cheap. Some may break down on the way, others last till the end. But the day has come at last when all the cars must set out.

III. Your letter has been a confirmation to me of the deep faith in the ultimate truths of humanity which we both try to serve and which sustains our being. I have tried to express how religion today as it exists in its prevalent institutionalised forms both in the West and the East has failed in its function to control and guide the forces of humanity; how the growth of nationalism and wide commerce of ideas through speeded-up communication have often augmented external differences instead of bringing humanity together. Development of organizing power, mastery over Nature's resources have subserved secret passions or the openly flaunted greed of unashamed national glorification. And yet I do not feel despondent about the future. For the great fact remains that man has never stopped in his urge for self-expression, in his brave quest of knowledge; not only so, there is today all over the world in spite of selfishness and unreason a greater *awareness* of truth. The fury of despotic tyranny, the denial of civic sanity and the violence with which the citadels of international federation are constantly assaulted, combine to betray an uncomfortable and increased consciousness in the mind of man of the inescapable responsibilities of humanity. It is this stirring of the human conscience to which we must look for a reassertion of man in religion, in political and economic affairs, in the spheres of education and social intercourse. It is apparent that innumerable individuals in every land are rising up vitalized by this faith, men and women who have suffered and sought the meaning of life and who are ready to stake their all for raising a new structure of human civilization on the foundation of international understanding and fellowship. In this fact lies the great hope of humanity—this emergence in every nation, in spite of repression and the suicidal fever of national war-mindedness, of the clean and radiant fires of individual consciousness. When I read some of the outstanding modern books published after the War I realize how the brighter spirits of young Europe are now alive to the challenge of our times. Nothing can be of greater joy to us in India than to find how unimpeachably great some of your scholars, historians, artists and literary men are in their fearless advocacy of truth, their passion for righteousness. In India, too, there is a great awakening everywhere, mainly under the inspiration of Mahatma Gandhi's singular purity of will and conduct, which is creating a new generation of clear-minded servers of our peoples. To these individuals of every land and race, these youthful spirits burning like clean flame on the altar of humanity, I offer my obeisance from the sunset-crested end of my road.

I feel proud that I have been born in this great Age. I know that it must take time before we can adjust our minds to a condition which is not only new, but almost exactly the opposite of the old. Let us announce to the world that the light of the morning has come, not for entrenching ourselves behind barriers, but for meeting in mutual understanding and trust on the common field of co-operation; never for nourishing a spirit of rejection, but for that glad acceptance which constantly carries in itself the giving out of the best that we have.

    Yours sincerely,
        RABINDRANATH TAGORE

To Secure the Peace of the World

CECIL RHODES

The last will of Cecil J. Rhodes provided a new approach to cross-cultural education. Here for the first time a private foundation was established for the express purpose of developing mutual understanding and good will among peoples through students. The principle of the need for study abroad was one that was soon used by other groups and governments.

THE LAST WILL AND TESTAMENT OF

CECIL JOHN RHODES *

(Dated July 1, 1899)

(5) *The Scholarships at Oxford.*

Whereas I consider that the education of young Colonists at one of the Universities in the United Kingdom is of great advantage to them for giving breadth to their views for their instruction in life and manners and for instilling into their minds the advantage to the Colonies as well as to the United Kingdom of the retention of the unity of the Empire.

And whereas in the case of young Colonists studying at a University in the United Kingdom I attach very great importance to the University having a residential system such as is in force at the Universities of Oxford and Cambridge for without it those students are at the most critical period of their lives left without any supervision.

And whereas there are at the present time 50 or more students from South Africa studying at the University of

---

* W. T. Stead, ed., *The Last Will and Testament of Cecil John Rhodes* (London, "Review of Review" Office, 1902), pp. 23-45.

Edinburgh many of whom are attracted there by its excellent medical school and I should like to establish some of the Scholarships hereinafter mentioned in that University but owing to its not having such a residential system as aforesaid I feel obliged to refrain from doing so. And whereas my own University the University of Oxford has such a system and I suggest that it should try and extend its scope so as if possible to make its medical school at least as good as that at the University of Edinburgh.

And whereas I also desire to encourage and foster an appreciation of the advantages which I implicitly believe will result from the union of the English-speaking peoples throughout the world and to encourage in the students from the United States of North America who will benefit from the American Scholarships to be established for the reason above given at the University of Oxford under this my Will an attachment to the country from which they have sprung but without I hope withdrawing them or their sympathies from the land of their adoption or birth.

Now therefore I direct my Trustees as soon as may be after my death and either simultaneously or gradually as they shall find convenient and if gradually then in such order as they shall think fit to establish for male students the Scholarships hereinafter directed to be established each of which shall be of the yearly value of 300 pounds and be tenable at any College in the University of Oxford for three consecutive academical years.

I direct my Trustees to establish certain Scholarships and these Scholarships I sometimes hereinafter refer to as "the Colonial Scholarships." . . .

I further direct my Trustees to establish additional Scholarships sufficient in number for the appropriation in the next following clause hereof directed and those Scholarships I sometimes hereinafter refer to as "the American Scholarships."

I appropriate two of the American Scholarships to each of the present States and Territories of the United States of North America. Provided that if any of the said

Territories shall in my lifetime be admitted as a State the scholarships appropriated to such Territory shall be appropriated to such State and that my Trustees may in their uncontrolled discretion withhold for such time as they shall think fit the appropriation of Scholarships to any Territory.

I direct that of the two Scholarships appropriated to a State or Territory not more than one shall be filled up in any year so that at no time shall more than two Scholarships be held for the same State or Territory.

[By Codicil executed in South Africa Mr. Rhodes after stating that the German Emperor had made instruction in English compulsory in German schools establishes fifteen Scholarships at Oxford (five in each of the first three years after his death) of 250 pounds each tenable for three years for students of German birth to be nominated by the German Emperor for "a good understanding between England Germany and the United States of America will secure the peace of the world and educational relations form the strongest tie."]

My desire being that the students who shall be elected to the Scholarships shall not be merely bookworms I direct that in the election of a student to a Scholarship regard shall be had to

(i) his literary and scholastic attainments

(ii) his fondness of and success in manly outdoor sports such as cricket football and the like

(iii) his qualities of manhood truth courage devotion to duty sympathy for the protection of the weak kindliness unselfishness and fellowship and

(iv) his exhibition during school days of moral force of character and of instincts to lead and to take an interest in his school-mates for those latter attributes will be likely in after-life to guide him to esteem the performance of public duty as his highest aim.

As mere suggestions for the guidance of those who will have the choice of students for the Scholarships I record that (i) my ideal qualified student would combine these

four qualifications in the proportions of three-tenths for
the first two-tenths for the second three-tenths for the
third and two-tenths for the fourth qualification so that
according to my ideas if the maximum number of marks
for any Scholarship were 200 they would be apportioned
as follows—60 to each of the first and third qualifications
and 40 to each of the second and fourth qualifications
(ii) the marks for the several qualifications would be
awarded independently as follows (that is to say) the
marks for the first qualification by examination for the
second and third qualifications respectively by ballot by
the fellow-students of the candidates and for the fourth
qualification by the head master of the candidate's
school and (iii) the results of the wards (that is to say
the marks obtained by each candidate for each qualification) would be sent as soon as possible for consideration
to the Trustees or to some person or persons appointed
to receive the same and the person or persons so appointed would ascertain by averaging the marks in
blocks of 20 marks each of all candidates the best ideal
qualified students.

No student shall be qualified or disqualified for election to a Scholarship on account of his race or religious
opinions.

Except in the cases of the four schools hereinbefore
mentioned the election to Scholarships shall be by the
Trustees after such (if any) consultation as they shall
think fit with the Minister having the control of education in such Colony, Province, State or Territory.

A qualified student who has been elected as aforesaid
shall within six calendar months after his election or as
soon thereafter as he can be admitted into residence or
within such extended time as my Trustees shall allow
Commence residence as an undergraduate at some college in the University of Oxford.

The scholarships shall be payable to him from the
time when he shall commence such residence.

I desire that the Scholars holding the scholarships
shall be distributed amongst the Colleges of the Univer-

sity of Oxford and not resort in undue numbers to one or more Colleges only.

Notwithstanding anything hereinbefore contained my Trustees may in their uncontrolled discretion suspend for such time as they shall think fit or remove any Scholar from his Scholarship.

In order that the Scholars past and present may have opportunities of meeting and discussing their experiences and prospects I desire that my Trustees shall annually give a dinner to the past and present Scholars able and willing to attend at which I hope my Trustees or some of them will be able to be present and to which they will I hope from time to time invite as guests persons who have shown sympathy with the views expressed by me in this my Will.

Cross-Cultural Education
through the Ages*

GUY S. MÉTRAUX

In this selection, Métraux sketches the historical development of cross-cultural education. This is an important study to consider at a time when 57,000 foreign students are on American campuses and nearly 10,000 Americans are abroad for educational purposes.

In tracing the origins of educational travel, the historian realizes that he must go back to the days of the Roman Republic, and he soon becomes aware of the fact that educational travel is related to various aspects of social life and that it has had an impact on social and economic development through the resultant diffusion of techniques and ideas. Moreover, he sees educational travel as a pattern that has evolved to meet changing climates of opinion, and that, as an apparently stable way to achieve certain purposes, it has, in reality, responded to various types of motivations. When he examines this movement in its contemporary setting, he is confronted by a complex subject which involves large numbers of people and an elaborate administrative setup. The purpose of this paper is to try to describe briefly the development of educational travel in Western history in its

* *International Social Science Bulletin*, Vol. VIII, No. 4 (Paris, UNESCO, 1956), pp. 577-584.

broadest social and cultural context, and to show succinctly this movement in its contemporary setting.[1]

The expression 'educational travel' involves two concepts: the adjective suggesting the acquisition of knowledge and the noun implying the dynamic process of migration. Both terms belong to two separate aspects of social organization; yet put together they are meaningful and used quite currently. The historian, however, should seek to place 'educational travel' in its proper social and cultural context and extract from its historical development its significance as a socially sanctioned way of achieving certain purposes.

Education implies for its development an elaborate social organization, a system of cultural values to be transmitted, a specialized personnel and institutions, as well as strong personal motivations. Migration, likewise, presupposes well-defined motivations, organization, resources and persons. If a society becomes conscious of the need for knowledge, skills or techniques that it does not possess, one way to acquire them is by resorting to temporary emigration to such areas as do possess them. Since it cannot migrate *in corpore* it is easier to encourage selected members of the group to go out to other groups where such knowledge is available and bring it back. It is at this point that education and migration coincide.[2]

In the paper I wrote for the Social Science Council in New York, I defined educational travel as a social process of acquiring knowledge of an intellectual or technical

[1] This article is partly based on the work of the author, *Exchange of Persons: The Evolution of Cross-Cultural Education* (Social Science Research Council, *Pamphlet* No. 9; New York, June 1952), 53 pp. For suggestions concerning educational travel in the Orient see David G. Mandelbaum, 'Comments', *Journal of Social Issues*, 1956, vol. 12, pp. 45-51.

[2] The importation of teachers and materials (books, journals, audio-visual devices, etc.) is also a way of compensating for the lack of knowledge in isolated areas. Contemporary educational travel is paralleled by significant efforts to increase the flow of educational materials across frontiers.

nature, under institutionalized conditions, outside one's own social and cultural environment.[3] This definition is only useful to the extent that it expresses the ambivalent character of educational travel which transcends the complex social patterns of 'education' and 'migration'.

Educational travel constitutes a *pattern* which has been remarkably persistent in Western history, and in the last one hundred years has been undergoing far-reaching changes which have increased its cultural and social significance. It has fulfilled two functions: the first which can be described as 'traditional' was to facilitate the acquisition of knowledge outside one's own environment; the second, and more recent, was to make use of educational travel to achieve socio-political and economic goals related to a certain climate of opinion to be achieved in international relations. These two functions overlap a good deal and, as we shall see, do not necessarily coincide.

The history of the transmission of ideas and techniques between complex civilizations is a subject that historians are beginning to study in detail. The role played by educational travel in this process can be more fully assessed once further documentary materials are brought to light.[4] Accordingly, in this general survey, the illustrations given of its main aspects at various periods of Western history do not represent the total picture of educational travel and should be assessed within their historical contexts.

3 G. S. Métraux, *op. cit.*, p. 1. Another definition was given recently: 'Cross-cultural education is the reciprocal process of learning and adjustment that occurs when individuals sojourn for educational purposes in a society that is culturally foreign to them, normally returning to their own society after a limited period. At the societal level, it is a process of cultural diffusion and change, involving temporary "exchange of persons" for training and experience.' M. Brewster Smith, 'Cross-Cultural Education as a Research Area', *Journal of Social Issues*, 1956, Vol. 12, p. 3.

4 An outstanding example of description and analysis of a chapter in the history of transmission of ideas and techniques is to be found in Joseph Needham, *Sciences and Civilization in China* (Cambridge, 1954), Vol. I, Chap. VII, 'Conditions of Travel of Scientific Ideas and Techniques between China and Europe', pp. 150-248.

The primary function of educational travel was the acquisition of knowledge and is best exemplified in the days of the Roman Republic when young men went to Greece to study literature, philosophy and the arts.[5] In the learned atmosphere of Greek cities, under teachers who had themselves worked under the great philosophers, the young men found the proper training that Rome at that time did not provide. What they learnt in Greece they brought back to Rome and contributed to the continuance of the Hellenistic tradition. Later, under the Empire, Greek teachers came to Rome and founded schools so that it was no longer necessary for Roman youths to leave the city for educational purposes.

After the downfall of the Empire and until the foundation of medieval universities, the movement of educational travel is difficult to isolate from the great migrations, the displacement of the political and religious centres, and the social changes that took place under the impact of Christianity. However, there was considerable educational travel in connexion with the diffusion of Christianity, through the founding of monasteries and the educational efforts of Charlemagne.

Much more important from our point of view is the foundation of the great centres of learning in the twelfth and thirteenth centuries to which students came from all over Europe. The concept of the university as an institution developed from the concentration around the teachers of students who created a special way of life and who received special privileges from the authorities.[6]

---

[5] Lloyd W. Daly, 'Roman Study Abroad', *American Journal of Philology*, 1950, Vol. 71, pp. 40-58. Athens was the foremost centre for Roman study abroad, although Rhodes, Pergamos and other centres were equally important. Alexandria played a considerable role in educational travel at that period. Cicero, Cæsar, Horace, Ovid studied in Greece. See, *inter alia*, Thomas Woody, *Life and Education in Early Societies* (New York, 1949), Chap. XIX, 'From Provincial to Cosmopolitan Culture', *passim;* also John W. H. Walden, *The Universities of Ancient Greece* (New York, 1909); also the studies of Professor Marrou of Paris on 'Education in Antiquity'.

[6] See Charles H. Haskins, *The Rise of Universities* (New York,

In certain universities, such as Paris, students were housed in colleges known then as 'nations'. This localization of learning was one of the characteristic features of medieval education. Thus Paris was known for its faculty of theology, Orleans and Bologna for Roman law, Salerno for medicine, etc. As Miss Helen Waddell has shown in her book *Wandering Scholars* 1927, students seeking proficiency in several disciplines travelled from university to university. Another feature of medieval higher education was the practice of awarding scholarships to deserving students who could not afford the cost of an education. These scholarships, provided by wealthy men, were to become one of the most widely accepted means to encourage study and played a key role in the development of educational travel .

With the establishment of more universities throughout Europe in the fourteenth, fifteenth and sixteenth centuries the need to travel away from one's own country lessened considerably. Basic teaching in the medieval curriculum became readily available and was, moreover, undergoing great changes under the stimulus of the Renaissance. With the Renaissance, however, educational travel took on importance as learning found new sources in the study of the humanities. The ferment of thought led to the foundation of academies and centres of discussion (such as the Platonic Academy of Marsiglio Ficino) and the presence of humanists in certain centres, such as Florence, Cambridge, Basle, etc., brought together scholars from all parts of Europe.

By evolving a liberal concept of education conducive to the good life, the humanists injected in educational travel a new motivation, making it an integral feature of the curriculum in liberal education. Travel became almost an end in itself designed to complement the process of acquiring an education. It enabled young people, said Montaigne, 'to bring back the characteristics of those nations and their manner of living, *and to rub*

1923), p. 13; also his *The Renaissance of the Twelfth Century* (Cambridge, Mass., 1927), p. 390; Marie Waxin, *Statut de l'étudiant étranger dans son développement historique* (Amiens, 1939), *passim.*

and file our wits against those of others'.[7] This idea appears to be entirely new in the formal training of youth;[8] but since the Renaissance it has become one of the prime causes for educational travel. It reflects two concepts: the usefulness of knowing other nations and their ways of life, and of testing one's own comportment in different environments. Educational travel motivated by this idea was highly important throughout the seventeenth and eighteenth centuries when it culminated in the 'Grand Tour', a period following formal training during which young men travelled fairly leisurely through Europe and, especially, in Italy.[9] Much student travel today is motivated by the belief that experience abroad is the final test, or the logical outcome, of formal training.

The significant aspect of this type of educational travel is that although connected with an educational process, it is no longer tied up with formal training in a specific discipline undergone at a centre of learning abroad especially selected for this purpose. It developed in societies that had established educational standards and did not need to draw specialized knowledge from abroad. It is a fact that the 'Grand Tour' was fashionable in those countries that had reached the highest literary, philosophical and scientific development (France, Great Britain, Germany). However, regions still in the periphery of Europe from the point of view of cultural development, such as the American colonies at that period or Russia of Peter the Great, sent their young men to Europe to acquire specialized knowledge essential for the economic, social and cultural development of their countries, but did not indulge in the fashionable 'Grand Tour' as such. This concept that travel experience was

7 *The Essays of Montaigne* (translation by George B. Ives; Cambridge, Mass., 1925), Vol. I, p. 205. Italics mine.

8 It is possible that a detailed analysis of Roman study abroad might show similar considerations.

9 E. S. Bates, *Touring in 1600: A Study in the Development of Travel as a Means of Education* (London, 1911): also R. S. Lambert, ed., *Grand Tour: A Journey in the Tracks of Aristocracy* (London, 1935).

a necessary complement to liberal education came to justify much student travelling in later periods.

During the nineteenth century educational travel in the two forms described above was considerably intensified. The development of communications made travel more accessible to more people and the opening of tourist facilities throughout Europe were an incentive. Such travel was perhaps less adventurous than in the eighteenth century, but it did not lack in educational values. Young men travelling during vacations in Italy, Switzerland and France became familiar figures in literature. At the same time, however, as a consequence of the demand for specialized technical knowledge created by scientific and technical progress achieved since the Industrial Revolution, a considerable number of young men came to work in certain fields of knowledge that were particularly well taught in Europe. These centres were endowed with laboratories, libraries and teaching personnel that could not yet be duplicated elsewhere. The students applied their new knowledge at home and became teachers in centres of learning thereby created. A good illustration of this is the development of medical science in the United States. Until the end of the nineteenth century the United States depended on Europe for the training of its medical personnel. Young American doctors studied at medical schools at Leyden, Edinburgh, London and later at Vienna, Munich and Paris, bringing back medical techniques which led to the formation of great American medical centres.[10] In turn, in the middle of the twentieth century, European doctors travelled to the United States to study in these centres.[11]

10 See Richard H. Shryock, *The Development of Modern Medicine: An Interpretation of the Social and Scientific Factors Involved* (New York, 1947) especially Chap. X, 'The Influence of French Medicine in Europe and America', and Chap. XII, 'Modern Medicine in Germany, 1830-1880'.

11 The historical development of medicine in the United States illustrates the steps suggested by an historian to describe the travel of techniques and ideas from centres of high development to outlying areas of lesser development. These steps were as follows: (a) reception from high development centre; (b) attendance at centre of high development (educational travel, from our point of view);

Toward the end of the nineteenth century there occurred in educational travel a new development which was to be significant in later years. Both in Japan and China, there was a real desire for modernization (equated at that period with Westernization) and a large number of young people went to Europe and America to acquire the techniques that would make it possible. This aspect of educational travel, which carried with it the desire to change the social and cultural basis of these societies, was fully recognized in the United States, and is best illustrated by the policy of Theodore Roosevelt who in 1909 directed the remission of a portion of the Boxer Indemnity Fund to the Chinese Government with the stipulation that scholarships would be established to bring Chinese students to America. In his message to Congress, the President said: 'This nation should help in every practicable way in the education of the Chinese people, so that the vast and populous Empire of China may gradually adapt itself to modern conditions. One way of doing this is by promoting the coming of Chinese students to this country and making it attractive to them to take courses at our universities and higher education institutions.'[12] A significant condition for applying for fellowships was that students should specialize in technical subjects (e.g., industrial arts, agriculture, mechanical engineering, mining, physics and chemistry, railway engineering and administration, architecture, etc.). Other subjects (for about 20 per cent of the students) were law and public administration.[13]

The traditional educational travel was thus widened to include the encouragement of cultural change in areas that remained outside the main stream of technical development and progress which had swept through

---

(c) dependence on centre of high development; (d) self-maintenance. See description of this process in Dixon R. Fox, *Ideas in Motion* (New York, 1935), Chap. I, 'Civilization in Transit', pp. 3-36 *passim*.

12 U. S. House of Representatives, *Remission of a Portion of the Chinese Indemnity: Message from the President of the United States* . . . , 60th Congress, 2nd session, House Doc. No. 1275 (1909), p. 6.

13 'The Remission of a Portion of the Chinese Indemnity', *American Journal of International Law*, 1909, Vol. 3, p. 456.

Europe and America during the nineteenth century. This pattern in educational travel, which was concerned with the general welfare of the countries involved rather than the personal development of individual students, culminated in various technical assistance programmes that were set up after World War II.[14]

Out of this new concept of educational travel concerned with the general welfare of a country developed yet another, and one that has dominated the position with regard to such travel today. As we have seen above Montaigne believed that it would be desirable for a young man to learn 'the characteristics of those nations and manners of living'. At the end of the nineteenth century Cecil Rhodes established a fund for fellowships, which has thereafter borne his name, to give young men from the British Empire, the United States and Germany the opportunity to study at Oxford. Although formal training in specified disciplines was one feature of these scholarships, the more important purpose was to instil in these scholars the realization of their common stake in life and in the destiny of their countries. The feeling of mutual understanding and good will created among these young men would, in turn, contribute to the hegemony of Anglo-American civilization. In the mind of the founder, the purely educational results of such fellowships were secondary to the greater political and economic goal that he had championed. As it turned out, the ambition of Cecil Rhodes was not fulfilled in the manner he had hoped: the cause of Anglo-American hegemony was dependent on other factors. But his plan to grant a liberal education in the Oxford tradition to young men from the far ends of the English-speaking world was carried out with great success.[15]

14 For a description of the place of educational travel within the structure of cultural change under technical assistance programmes, see Margaret Mead, ed., *Cultural Patterns and Technical Change* (Paris, Unesco, 1953), Chap. II, 'The International Setting of Technical Change'.

15 See *inter alia*, W. T. Stead, ed., *The Last Will and Testament of Cecil John Rhodes* (London, 1902); George R. Parkin, *The Rhodes Scholarships* (Boston, 1912): Frank Aydelotte, *The American Rhodes Scholarships: A Review of the First Forty Years* (Princeton, 1946).

However, this motivation for educational travel, which transcended the simple quest for knowledge and was meant to create a climate of mutual understanding and good will among students of varying backgrounds, became one of the primary reasons for the promotion of international travel in the years preceding World War I and after. About 1910 Nicholas Murray Butler and Elihu Root had persuaded Andrew Carneigie to set up a special foundation for the promotion of peace. This foundation, known as the Carnegie Endowment for International Peace, had as one of its functions that of finding ways to 'cultivate friendly feelings between the inhabitants of different countries and to increase the knowledge and understanding of each other of the several nations'.[16]

During the war a highly effective propaganda stressed the community of interests among the Allied powers and considerable effort was made to assist war-devastated areas, both materially and spiritually. After the war, this spirit of good will led to the establishment of international governmental and non-governmental organizations for the promotion of international education.[17] Most of the organizations included primary and secondary schoolchildren in their programmes of educational travel. An illustration of the aims of such organizations is the following quotation from a publication of the International Institute of Intellectual Co-operation: 'Foreign travel has always been regarded as one of the indispensable aids to the training and education of youth. Today, however, school travel is assigned a *new and special* role —that of contributing to the 'rapprochement' between nations. It is generally recognized that school children who are sent on visits to foreign countries are given an opportunity not only of improving their knowledge of a foreign language but also of coming into contact with another civilization and of establishing personal bonds of

[16] Nicholas Murray Butler, *The International Mind: An Argument for the Judicial Settlement of International Disputes* (New York, 1912), p. 82.

[17] Pedro Rossello, *Forerunner of the International Bureau of Education* (London, ca. 1944-45), 120 pp.

friendship *which will ultimately contribute to the development of a spirit of goodwill and understanding between peoples.*[18]

It is in this climate of opinion that the terms 'student exchange' and 'student interchange' became generally accepted to describe educational travel. It led to a series of bilateral agreements among nations designed to increase cultural relations in which actual 'exchange' of students was quite prominent. By 1929 there were in Europe alone over 700 private and official organizations which in one way or another promoted cultural relations and student exchanges.[19]

After World War II, the promotion of educational travel to develop mutual understanding and good will continued to be one of the primary motivations for the donation of fellowships for study abroad. The purpose of many scholarships awarded by the United States Government is stated as follows: 'Awards are made to increase mutual understanding between the peoples of the U.S.A. and the peoples of other countries.'[20]

A derivative purpose of the pattern described above is the promotion of exchanges of students and other persons with the intention of influencing their political views and thereby modifying the climate of opinion in

[18] International Institute of Intellectual Co-operation, *International Understanding through Youth: Interchange and Travel of School Pupils* (Paris, 1933), p. 11. Italics mine.

[19] International Institute of Intellectual Co-operation, *University Exchanges in Europe: Handbook of Institutions and Measures in all European Countries to Facilitate the Work of Professors, Students and Teachers Abroad* (Paris, 1929 and several later editions), also available in French and in German.

[20] Unesco, *Study Abroad*, Vol. VII (1955), A 1567 to A 1572, and A 1574 to A 1577. A 1573 is described as follows: 'to enable recipients to undertake graduate study abroad and to become acquainted with other peoples and customs, *thereby* furthering international understanding'. Italics ours. Explaining to the readers of the *New York Times* the activities in student exchanges under the Fulbright Act, Senator Fulbright wrote: '. . . the purpose of the program is not the advancement of science nor the promotion of scholarship. These are by-products of a program whose primary aim is international understanding.' (J. William Fulbright, 'Open Doors, Not Iron Curtains', *New York Times Magazine*, 5 August 1951, p. 18).

their native lands. This has been particularly true of certain programmes organized before World War II and in the late forties. This conception has been described as follows: Lasting changes must be brought from within; to stimulate and encourage this process requires the utmost tact and understanding. It is possible to help along the process of cultural rehabilitation and of democratization by offering services known to be both needed and desired, such as exchanges of personnel and materials.[21]

The overt use of educational travel to create a climate of opinion favourable to world peace, or to implement certain objectives in international relations, is considerably removed from its traditional objectives and suggests that cross-cultural education as a social institution is highly responsive to changing climates of opinion.

Available evidence of the success of the objectives of educational travel—other than the traditional one—that grew out of the two world wars is not conclusive. This is true of the politico-social objectives for scholarships established before World War II to promote good will, although it seems certain that individual students greatly benefited from such travel, either by broadening their general experience or by acquiring greater proficiency in a foreign language.[22] Also in a recent publication, it has been shown that a group of German visitors to the United States did not greatly modify their opinion of America, although some changes in attitudes towards their own country were noted.[23] Further, in evaluating the results achieved by a group of Japanese students brought to the United States under official auspices, one finding was that a common cause of failure

21 Harold E. Snyder, 'Voluntary Exchanges with Occupied Areas —Why and How?', *Educational and Psychological Measurement,* 1949, Vol. 9, No. 3, p. 642.

22 Theodosia Hewlett, 'A Decade of International Fellowships: A Survey of Impressions of American and Foreign Ex-Fellows', Institute of International Education *Bulletin,* Series 11, No. 2 (New York, 1 June 1930).

23 Jeanne Watson and Ronald Lippitt, *Learning Across Cultures: A Study of Germans Visiting America* (Ann Arbor, 1955), Chap. 8, 'Attitude Changes: Summary and Conclusions', *passim.*

was the conflict between the official aims of the programme and the students' desire to pursue purely
academic studies.[24] A pamphlet published in 1955 emphasized again this discrepancy in objectives.[25] The
awareness in responsible circles that such a conflict exists
in educational travel may lead to the reconsideration of
the aims and organization of some programmes to bring
them closer to the original purpose of such travel, that
of facilitating the acquisition of knowledge and enabling
young men to complement their formal training.

The main features that characterize educational travel
today as compared to earlier forms show how greatly the
pattern has evolved. In recent years these features are:
(a) the large number of academic and technical personnel involved; (b) the existence of special organizations
for the promotion and availability of a large number of
scholarships; (c) the important place of studies not connected with the academic pattern in the traditional
sense; and (d) its special function of promoting culture
contacts and changes. These characteristics will be ana-
lysed in the other papers reproduced in this issue. It
will suffice here to say that the very complex nature of
cross-cultural education, the large number of persons involved and its potential impact on society have aroused
the interest of social scientists who are developing an
important body of information on all aspects of educational travel.[26] The literature on educational travel is
considerable although, unfortunately, it is a subject that
has not been dealt with sufficiently by historians.[27]

24 Office of the U. S. Secretary of the Army, *Evaluation of Japanese Student Program*, 6. April, 1951, p. 7.

25 Committee on Educational Interchange Policy, *The Goals of
Student Exchange: An Analysis of Goals of Programs for Foreign
Students* (New York, January 1955).

26 An inventory of research in cross-cultural education listed at
the beginning of 1956 23 projects; for further details see M.
Brewster Smith, 'A Perspective for Further Research on Cross-Cultural Education', *Journal of Social Issues*, 1956, Vol. 12, pp. 56-68.

27 U. S. Office of Education, Department of Health, Education
and Welfare, *A Partial Bibliography Related to International Education* (Washington, D. C., 1954), 104 pp. A recent sociological study
of educational travel indicates its complexity and suggests its im-

It is probable that studies of the movement as they are being conducted now will contribute to a greater understanding of its true functions. They will probably result in the reconsideration of certain fundamental aspects of the movement by those responsible for its promotion. In the meanwhile, educational travel will in all likelihood continue as a channel of communication between peoples, as a means to acquire knowledge and as a valuable way to complement formal training by providing young men with an opportunity to study other cultures at first hand. This experience could lead to a reassessment of their own cultures and might result in culture changes. Historians and social scientists of the future will be able to assess the significance of the movement for our world.

---

pact both on the individual and society. More studies of this type are needed to assess cross-cultural education in all of its aspects. See John and Ruth Hill Useem, *The Western-educated Man in India: a Study of his Social Roles and Influence* (New York, Dryden Press, 1955, 237 p.).

Education and Colonial Dependencies*

ISAAC L. KANDEL

For many decades it was customary for metropolitan European countries to introduce their own educational systems in colonial dependencies. Today many newly independent countries, formerly colonies, are attempting to build educational systems that will meet their particular long-range goals and immediate needs.

The demands on such former colonies are great. There is the problem of mass education versus education of an elite. Manpower studies are indicating the type of trained individuals needed if economic development is to take place. Educational leaders are examining their educational systems to determine the type of system that can meet their needs and yet at the same time be within their traditional patterns. The problem of conflicting traditions, in terms both of cultural and of educational patterns, is one that is felt throughout the world in the less-developed societies. In his essay, written nearly thirty years ago, Professor Kandel discusses this crucial question, so real today—Adaptation or assimilation?

* * *

There is today no more challenging field of activity in education than that of extending its provision to parts of the world which are gradually being drawn within the influences of western civilization. This does not mean either that the peoples concerned have not had

* Isaac L. Kandel, "Introduction," *Educational Yearbook of the International Institute of Teachers College, Columbia University, 1931* (New York, Bureau of Publications, Teachers College, Columbia University, 1932), pp. ix-xv.

some type of education of their own or that the powers concerned in their welfare have not already organized systems of education for them. Generally, however, the type of education that indigenous peoples have themselves developed from time immemorial is no longer adapted to promote their survival once they come into contact with modern civilization, while the educational systems devised for them have been nothing more than transplantations of systems which have been developed under entirely different conditions and imposed without reference to the needs of the peoples concerned.

So long as the emphasis in education was mainly on literacy and the idea prevailed that training in the three R's would be accompanied by moral improvement, there was some justification in transplanting to alien civilizations a type of education which was regarded as beneficial under all circumstances. This rather than the desire to forge chains of imperialistic control explains the transfer of English education to India, French education to French colonies, and American education to the Philippines and Porto Rico. The educational unrest in India, although closely interwoven with the nationalist movement, is equally a manifestation of the failure of the attempt to transplant the educational system of one country to another. In the same way the results of the surveys of the educational systems of the Philippines and Porto Rico, after an experiment conducted over a quarter of a century, revealed the failure of the attempt of the United States to give to these dependencies what was at the time of their introduction regarded as the most advanced experiment in democratic education.

The powers which adopted the policy of transplantation or assimilation in education could not be charged with shortsightedness at a time when education in literacy was regarded as a universal panacea for social, moral, and economic ills. Changes in policy could be brought about only in two ways: first, by the realization of the failure of an education in literacy; second, by the recognition in the home countries themselves that education is not a commodity that can be standardized, that it is governed by the social traditions and ideals and by the environment which it serves, and that it is broader than book learning.

Evidences of failure were not difficult to find. Book learning, and particularly learning from books which were based on alien cultures and environments, it was soon discovered, resulted in a species of psittacism, in an external polish, which was of no value in itself and only resulted in rendering the learner unhappy in his own environment. The premium placed on book learning and the neglect of any other type of education weaned the native away from his everyday work; the man who could read and write felt it beneath his dignity to engage in manual occupations. The rudiments of an elementary education were just as disintegrating among backward peoples as the expansion of secondary education among advanced peoples in so far as they led to aspirations for "white collar" jobs. That considerable mischief has already been done by the assimilationist policy can be abundantly proved.

And yet nothing better could have been expected so long as education everywhere was dominated by bookishness. It was not until the present century that the concept of education was broadened and the educative value of practical instruction both as a method of learning and in its social implications began to be recognized in the leading countries of Europe and in the United States. With the gradual breakdown of the traditional ideal of education, assimilation has given place to adaptation to social and economic needs as the starting-point for an educational system. That the new ideal is progressing slowly is indicated in the survival of the traditional aims of academic study in the field of secondary education for all. The attitude of peoples living under western civilization to secondary education is paralleled by the attitude of backward peoples to elementary education.

Education in colonial dependencies is at present at the crossroads. As the civilized world is gradually extending its boundaries and the significance of educating vast millions of peoples who have hitherto been isolated and content with their own customs, traditions, and occupations is being realized, ruling powers are beginning to consider the educational problems involved as they never did before. In the following pages it is clear that they are confronted with the choice between the policy of assimilation or of adaptation. A study of the education provided in the French colonies, where the systems in the past have been extensions of the system of the mother country with its emphasis on French culture, certificates, and diplomas, reveals that a stage has been reached where the same choice has to be made. The discussions and conferences on education which took place in 1931 in connection with the French Colonial Exposition revealed the weaknesses and strength of the French practices and brought to the surface the problems with which educators are confronted in the French colonies. That the problems are not confined to France is indicated in the establishment of the Advisory Committee of the British Colonial Office, in the creation of the Institute of Education at the University of London, by the surveys of education in the Philippines and in Porto Rico, and the increasing number of students who are drawn each year to Teachers College, Columbia University, attracted not for the purpose of studying American education primarily, but to acquaint themselves with the meaning of education as adaptation.

The introductory article by Professor C. T. Loram, which follows, reveals the problems with which the educator among backward peoples is confronted. Here may be seen the change in the concept of education which has taken place in the last twenty-five years. It opens up problems which have hitherto been almost completely ignored. The policy of assimilation, proceeding on the assumption that the type of education which was good at home is also the best for the native living hitherto under primitive conditions, was content to transfer the education of the home country to the dependency. The policy of adaptation is confronted with a vast array of problems—language of instruction, language of intercourse, ethnology, local customs and mores, health, social training, vocational training, provision and maintenance of schools, higher education, religious instruction, primitive arts and crafts, and so on.

Education in colonial dependencies cannot be regarded as an isolated matter in which the educator in more established centers has no concern. Actually these areas, because from some points of view conditions are simpler and more easily subject to analysis, constitute laboratories in which the new philosophy of education can be tested perhaps better than under the complicated conditions of Europe and the United States where certain traditions have long become established. It is not improbable that experimentation with peoples who are, as it were, just beginning to go to school will in time have important contributions to make to educational theory in general. The part played by missionary organizations in the development of education is referred to in all the articles which follow. Because they have opportunities which are broader in some respects than formal education and are concerned not only with backward peoples but with civilizations older than the European, the problems confronting missionary educators will be dealt with separately in a forthcoming Yearbook.

There is included in the present volume an article on extra-territorial activities of France in education, which furnishes an example of a system of promoting international cultural exchange which is almost unparalleled in other countries. The Office of Special Inquiries and Reports of the English Board of Education arranges for the exchange of teachers between England and her dominions and between England and France. The Institute of International Education serves as a liaison agent between the United States and foreign countries and arranges the exchange of students and teachers. France, however, through the Office National des Universités et Écoles Françaises, goes further and through her cultural outposts in all parts of the world illustrates what might be done for international understanding if the practice were adopted by other countries.

A Bold New Program:
Point Four*

HARRY S. TRUMAN

The Point Four proposal by President Truman represented a new step in international affairs. Here for the first time was the statement that it was the responsibility of the more industrially advanced nations to share their knowledge with the less developed societies. While such a movement had already been recognized by the United Nations, President Truman's proposal placed an added responsibility on each of the industrialized countries of the West. This call for a sharing of knowledge has been followed by other European countries developing their own technical assistance programs.

INAUGURAL ADDRESS OF THE PRESIDENT

* * *

Fourth, we must embark on a bold new program for making the benefits of our scientific advances and industrial progress available for the improvement and growth of underdeveloped areas.

More than half the people of the world are living in conditions approaching misery. Their food is inadequate. They are victims of disease. Their poverty is a handicap and a threat both to them and to more prosperous areas.

For the first time in history, humanity possesses the knowledge and the skill to relieve the suffering of these people.

* *The Department of State Bulletin*, Vol. XX, No. 500 (Washington, D. C., Government Printing Office, Jan. 30, 1949), pp. 123-126.

The United States is pre-eminent among nations in the development of industrial and scientific techniques. The material resources which we can afford to use for the assistance of other peoples are limited. But our imponderable resources in technical knowledge are constantly growing and are inexhaustible.

I believe that we should make available to peace-loving peoples the benefits of our store of technical knowledge in order to help them realize their aspirations for a better life. And, in cooperation with other nations, we should foster capital investment in areas needing development.

Our aim should be to help the free peoples of the world, through their own efforts, to produce more food, more clothing, more materials for housing, and more mechanical power to lighten their burdens.

We invite other countries to pool their technological resources in this undertaking. Their contributions will be warmly welcomed. This should be a cooperative enterprise in which all nations work together through the United Nations and its specialized agencies wherever practicable. It must be a world-wide effort for the achievement of peace, plenty, and freedom.

With the cooperation of business, private capital, agriculture, and labor in this country, this program can greatly increase the industrial activity of other nations and can raise substantially their standards of living.

Such new economic developments must be devised and controlled to benefit the peoples of the areas in which they are established. Guarantees to the investor must be balanced by guarantees in the interest of the people whose resources and whose labor go into these developments.

The old imperialism—exploitation for foreign profit— has no place in our plans. What we envisage is a program of development based on the concepts of democratic fair-dealing.

All countries, including our own, will greatly benefit from a constructive program for the better use of the world's human and natural resources. Experience shows that our commerce with other countries expands as they progress industrially and economically.

Greater production is the key to prosperity and peace. And the key to greater production is a wider and more vigorous application of modern scientific and technical knowledge.

Only by helping the least fortunate of its members to help themselves can the human family achieve the decent, satisfying life that is the right of all people.

Democracy alone can supply the vitalizing force to stir the peoples of the world into triumphant action, not only against their human oppressors, but also against their ancient enemies—hunger, misery, and despair.

On the basis of these four major courses of action we hope to help create the conditions that will lead eventually to personal freedom and happiness for all mankind.

If we are to be successful in carrying out these policies, it is clear that we must have continued prosperity in this country and we must keep ourselves strong.

Slowly but surely we are weaving a world fabric of international security and growing prosperity.

We are aided by all who wish to live in freedom from fear—even by those who live today in fear under their own governments.

We are aided by all who want relief from the lies of propaganda—who desire truth and sincerity.

We are aided by all who desire self-government and a voice in deciding their own affairs.

We are aided by all who long for economic security—for the security and abundance that men in free societies can enjoy.

We are aided by all who desire freedom of speech, freedom of religion, and freedom to live their own lives for useful ends.

Our allies are the millions who hunger and thirst after righteousness.

In due time, as our stability becomes manifest, as more and more nations come to know the benefits of democracy and to participate in growing abundance, I believe that those countries which now oppose us will abandon their delusions and join with the free nations of the world in a just settlement of international differences.

Events have brought our American democracy to new influence and new responsibilities. They will test our courage, our devotion to duty, and our concept of liberty.

But I say to all men, what we have achieved in liberty, we will surpass in greater liberty.

Steadfast in our faith in the Almighty, we will advance toward a world where man's freedom is secure.

To that end we will devote our strength, our resources, and our firmness of resolve. With God's help, the future of mankind will be assured in a world of justice, harmony, and peace.

The Soviet–American Cultural
Exchange Agreement*

*"Cultural relations" programs were originally con-
ceived as arrangements for communication and exchange in the arts and letters. Today they have
been extended to include many other areas, as illustrated by the wide range of activities covered by
the recent Lacy–Zaroubin agreement.*

AGREEMENT BETWEEN THE UNITED STATES OF AMERICA
AND THE UNION OF SOVIET SOCIALIST REPUBLICS ON
EXCHANGES IN THE CULTURAL, TECHNICAL, AND EDUCA-
TIONAL FIELDS

By agreement between the Governments of the United
States of America and the Union of Soviet Socialist Republics, delegations headed on the United States side by
Ambassador William S. B. Lacy and on the Soviet side
by Ambassador G. N. Zaroubin conducted negotiations
in Washington from October 28, 1957 to January 27,
1958, with regard to cultural, technical, and educational
exchanges between the United States of America and the
Union of Soviet Socialist Republics. As a result of these
negotiations, which have been carried on in a spirit of
mutual understanding, the United States and the Soviet
Union have agreed to provide for the specific exchanges
which are set forth in the following sections during 1958
and 1959 in the belief that these exchanges will contribute significantly to the betterment of relations between
the two countries, thereby contributing to a lessening of
international tensions.

* U. S. Congress House, *Government Programs In International
Education*, Forty-Second Report of the Committee on Government Operations, 85th Congress, Second Session, H. R. No. 2712,
(Washington, D. C., Government Printing Office, 1959), pp. 223-
229.

SECTION I. GENERAL

(1) The visits and exchanges enumerated in the following sections are not intended to be exclusive of others which may be arranged by the two countries or undertaken by their citizens.

(2) The exchanges provided for in the following sections shall be subject to the Constitution and applicable laws and regulations in force in the respective countries. It is understood that both parties will use their best efforts to have these exchanges effected in accordance with the following sections.

SECTION II. EXCHANGES OF RADIO AND TELEVISION BROADCASTS

(1) Both parties will provide for an exchange of radio and television broadcasts on the subjects of science, technology, industry, agriculture, education, public health, and sports.

(2) Both parties will provide for regular exchanges of radio and television programs, which will include the exchange of transcribed classical, folk, and contemporary musical productions on magnetic tape and records; the exchange of filmed musical, literary, theatrical, and similar television productions.

(3) For the purpose of strengthening mutual understanding and developing friendly relations between the United States and the Union of Soviet Socialist Republics, both parties agree to organize from time to time an exchange of broadcasts devoted to discussion of such international political problems as may be agreed upon between the two parties. The details of the exchanges shall be agreed upon at the working level.[1]

1 By exchange of letters, dated January 27, 1958, the following amendment was agreed to:

"With respect to paragraph 3 of section II of the Agreement signed this date, it is the understanding of both parties to the Agreement that the texts of such broadcasts shall be exchanged in advance and discussed at the working level. In the event that either party shall consider that the effect of any such broadcast will not contribute to a betterment of relations between the United States

(4) Both parties will provide for an exchange of samples of equipment for sound recording and telecasting and their technical specifications.

(5) Both parties will provide for an exchange of delegations of specialists in 1958 to study the production of radio and television programs, the technique of sound recording, the equipment of radio and television studios, and the manufacture of films, recording tape, tape recorders, and records.

SECTION III. EXCHANGE OF GROUPS OF SPECIALISTS IN INDUSTRY, AGRICULTURE, AND MEDICINE

(1) Both parties agree to provide for an exchange of delegations in 1958 in the fields of iron and steel, mining (iron ore), and plastics industry. Both parties agree as to the desirability of arranging additional exchanges in industry during 1958-59.

(2) Both sides will provide for the exchange of delegations of specialists in agriculture, the American side receiving during 1958-59 nine delegations of Soviet specialists in the following fields: mechanization of agriculture, animal husbandry, veterinary science, mixed feeds, cotton growing, agricultural construction and electrification, horticulture (including vegetable growing), hydro-engineering (irrigation) and reclamation, and forestry, lumbering, and millwork. In 1958-59 the Soviet side will receive nine American delegations of specialists in the following fields: the study of agricultural crops, veterinary science, soil use and the use of water resources (irrigation and drainage), mechanization of agriculture, agricultural economics (excluding distribution of agricultural products), cotton growing and plant physiology, sheep raising, biological control of agricultural pests, and forestry, lumbering, and millwork.

Details of the exchanges will be agreed upon by representatives of the Department of State of the United States of America and of the Embassy of the Union of Soviet Socialist Republics in the United States of America.

of America and the Union of Soviet Socialist Republics, the exchange of such broadcast shall not take place."

(3) Both parties agree to provide for the exchange in 1958-1959 of 8 medical delegations of 5 to 6 specialists for periods of 2 to 6 weeks to become familiar with research and achievement in the following fields: New antibiotics, microbiology, physiology and pharmacology of the nervous system, radiobiology, biochemistry, metabolic diseases, endocrinology, community and industrial hygiene.

Both parties recognize the desirability of providing for an exchange of delegations in the field of the manufacture of medical apparatus and instruments.

(4) Both parties agree in principle to provide for an exchange in 1958 of delegations of specialists in fisheries.

SECTION IV. VISITS BY REPRESENTATIVES OF CULTURAL, CIVIC, YOUTH, AND STUDENT GROUPS

(1) For the purpose of establishing contacts, exchanging experiences, and becoming more familiar with the public and cultural life of both countries, the Soviet side will arrange to invite to the Union of Soviet Socialist Republics during 1958 groups of American writers (5-6 persons), composers (5-6 persons), painters and sculptors (3-4 persons). In 1958, the United States side reciprocally will arrange to invite similar Soviet groups to visit the United States.

(2) Both parties will provide for the exchange in 1958-59 of delegations of representatives of youth and delegations of women in various professions.

(3) Both parties agree to provide for an exchange of delegations of student and youth newspaper editors in 1958-59.

(4) Both parties will promote the development and strengthening of friendly contacts between Soviet and American cities.

SECTION V. EXCHANGE OF VISITS OF DELEGATIONS OF MEMBERS OF THE UNITED STATES CONGRESS AND DEPUTIES OF THE SUPREME SOVIET OF THE U.S.S.R.

The proposal to exchange delegations of members of the United States Congress and deputies of the Supreme

Soviet of the Union of Soviet Socialist Republics will be subject to further discussion between the two parties.

SECTION VI. JOINT CONFERENCES OF UNITED STATES AND U.S.S.R. ORGANIZATIONS

The desirability of agreement to hold joint conferences of interparliamentary groups in 1958 and 1959 or meetings of representatives of the United States and Soviet associations for the United Nations and UNESCO[2] is a matter for the organizations concerned.

SECTION VII. COOPERATION IN THE FIELD OF CINEMATOGRAPHY

Recognizing the importance of developing mutual cooperation between the United States of America and the Union of Soviet Socialist Republics in the field of motion pictures, both parties have agreed to the following:

(1) To make provisions for the sale and purchase of motion pictures by the film industries of both countries on the principles of equality and on mutually acceptable financial terms. Toward this end, not later than January 1958, Sovexportfilm will enter into contract with representatives of the motion-picture industry in the United States, to be approved by the Department of State of the United States, for the purpose of the sale and purchase of films in 1958.

(2) To arrange for the holding simultaneously in the United States of America and the Union of Soviet Republics of film premieres (American films in the Union of Soviet Socialist Republics and Soviet films in the United States of America, respectively), inviting to these premieres leading personalities of the film industries of both countries.

(3) To carry out in 1958 an exchange of 12 to 15 documentary films in accordance with a list to be mutually agreed upon by the two parties. On the Soviet side the exchange of documentary films will be carried out by

2 United Nations Educational, Scientific, and Cultural Organization.

Sovexportfilm, such films to be recorded in the English language, and for the United States of America by the United States Information Agency, such films to be recorded in the Russian language.

(4) In the second half of 1958 to provide for carrying out for a period of up to 1 month an interchange of delegations of leading motion-picture personalities, scenario writers, and technical personnel to be approved by each side for the purpose of becoming acquainted with experiences in the production of motion pictures in the respective countries.

(5) To recognize the desirability and usefulness of organizing joint production of artistic, popular-science, and documentary films, and of the conducting, not later than May 1958, of concrete negotiations between Soviet film organizations and United States film companies on this subject, such United States companies to be approved by the Department of State of the United States. The subject matter of the films will be mutually agreed upon by the two parties.

(6) To recommend to the appropriate United States organizations the making of arrangements for the holding of a Soviet Film Week in the United States in 1958 and to recommend to the appropriate motion-picture organizations of the Soviet Union the making of arrangements for the holding of a United States Film Week in the Soviet Union in 1958, and to envision the participation in these film weeks of delegations from each side numbering 3 or 4 motion-picture personalities for a period of 2 weeks.

(7) To recognize the desirability of producing feature films, documentary films, and concert films for television or nontheatrical showing in the United States by Soviet motion-picture organizations and the producing of similar films by appropriate United States organizations for television or nontheatrical showing in the Soviet Union. Additional concrete negotiations on this question will be carried on between the Department of State of the United States and the Soviet Embassy in the United States of America.

(8) To designate a standing committee of 4 members,

2 from the United States and 2 from the Soviet Union, the powers of which will be for a period of 1 year and which will meet once in Moscow and once in Washington during that year to examine problems which may arise in connection with the implementation of the provisions of this section. The authority of this committee may be extended by mutual agreement.

SECTION VIII. EXCHANGE OF THEATRICAL, CHORAL, AND CHOREOGRAPHIC GROUPS, SYMPHONY ORCHESTRAS, AND ARTISTIC PERFORMERS

(1) The Ministry of Culture of the Union of Soviet Socialist Republics will invite the Philadelphia Symphony Orchestra to visit the Soviet Union in May or June 1958 and will send the ballet troupe of the Bolshoi Theatre of the Soviet Union, numbering 110-120 persons, to the United States in 1959 for a period of 1 month.

(2) The Ministry of Culture of the Union of Soviet Socialist Republics, on the basis of an existing agreement with Hurok Attractions, Inc., and the Academy of the National Theatre and Drama, will send two Soviet performers—E. Gilels, pianist, and L. Kogan, violinist—to the United States in January-April 1958, and will invite two American soloists, B. Thebom, vocalist, and L. Warren, vocalist, to visit the Soviet Union.

(3) The Ministry of Culture of the Union of Soviet Socialist Republics will send Soviet vocalists I. Petrov, P. Lisitsian, and Z. Dolukhanova, as well as I. Bezrodni, violinist, and V. Ashkenazi, pianist, to the United States, and will invite R. Peters, vocalist, L. Stokowski, conductor, and others to visit the Soviet Union.

(4) The Ministry of Culture of the Union of Soviet Socialist Republics, in accordance with an agreement with Hurok Attractions, Inc., will send the State Folk Dance Ensemble of the Union of Soviet Socialist Republics to the United States in April-May 1958 and will consider inviting a leading American theatrical or choreographic group to the Soviet Union in 1959.

(5) The Soviet side will send the red banner song and dance ensemble of the Soviet Army or the choreographic

ensemble Beriozka to the United States in the fourth quarter of 1958 and invite one of the leading American choreographic groups to visit the Soviet Union.

SECTION IX, VISITS BY SCIENTISTS

(1) The Academy of Sciences of the Union of Soviet Socialist Republics and the National Academy of Sciences of the United States will, on a reciprocal basis, provide for the exchange of groups or individual scientists and specialists for delivering lectures and holding seminars on various problems of science and technology.

(2) The Academy of Sciences of the Union of Soviet Socialist Republics and the National Academy of Sciences of the United States will, on a reciprocal basis, provide for the exchange of scientific personnel and specialists for the purpose of conducting joint studies and for specialization for a period of up to 1 year.

(3) The details of exchanges mentioned in paragraphs (1) and (2) will be agreed upon directly between the presidents of the Academy of Sciences of the Union of Soviet Socialist Republics and the National Academy of Sciences of the United States in Moscow in the early part of 1958.

(4) The Ministry of Health of the Union of Soviet Socialist Republics will send in 1958 to the United States a group of Soviet medical scientists (3 to 4 persons) for a period of 2 to 3 weeks to deliver lectures and exchange experiences and will receive a similar group of United States medical scientists to deliver lectures and exchange experiences at the institute of the Academy of Medical Sciences of the Union of Soviet Socialist Republics and at medical institutes in Moscow, Leningrad, and Kiev.

(5) In 1958 the Ministry of Agriculture of the Union of Soviet Socialist Republics will, on a reciprocal basis, invite United States scientists to visit the Union of Soviet Socialist Republics for the purpose of delivering lectures and exchanging experiences in the fields of biology, selection, pedigreed stockbreeding, agrotechny, mechanization of agriculture, stockbreeding, and others.

SECTION X, EXCHANGE OF UNIVERSITY DELEGATIONS

(1) Both parties will provide for the exchange in 1958 of 4 delegations of university professors and instructors for a period of 2 to 3 weeks in the fields of natural sciences, engineering education, and liberal arts, and the study of the systems of higher education in the United States and the Soviet Union, each delegation to consist of from 5 to 8 persons.

(2) Both parties will provide for an exchange of delegations of professors and instructors between Moscow and Columbia Universities and Leningrad and Harvard Universities. Further exchanges of delegations of professors and instructors of other universities of the United States of America and the Union of Soviet Socialist Republics shall be decided upon as appropriate by both parties.

(3) Both parties will provide for an exchange of students between Moscow and Leningrad Universities, on the one hand, and United States Universities, on the other, amounting to 20 persons on each side for the period of the academic year 1958-59. For the academic year 1959–60, the number will be 30. The composition of the student groups shall be determined by each side.

(4) Both parties will provide for an exchange of delegations of educators (8 to 10 persons) for a period of 30 days in the latter part of 1958.

SECTION XI, EXCHANGE OF INDIVIDUAL ATHLETES AND ATHLETIC TEAMS

Both parties will provide for an exchange of individual athletes and athletic teams and in 1958-59 will provide for the holding of the following contests in the United States and in the Union of Soviet Socialist Republics:

(1) Basketball games between representative men's and women's teams to be held in the Soviet Union in April 1958.

(2) Basketball games between representative men's

and women's teams to be held in the United States in 1959.

(3) Wrestling matches between representative teams to be held in the United States in February 1958.

(4) Wrestling matches between representative teams to be held in the Soviet Union in 1959.

(5) Track and field contests between representative teams to be held in the Soviet Union in July 1958.

(6) Track and field contests between representative teams to be held in the United States in 1959.

(7) Weight-lifting contests between representative teams to be held in the United States in May 1958.

(8) Canadian hockey games between representative teams to be held in the Soviet Union in March-April 1958.

(9) Chess tournaments between representative teams to be held in the United States in 1958.

The details of these exchanges of athletes and athletic teams as well as financial arrangements for these exchanges shall be discussed between appropriate American and Soviet sports organizations.

SECTION XII, DEVELOPMENT OF TOURISM

Both parties will promote the development of tourism.

SECTION XIII, EXCHANGE OF EXHIBITS AND PUBLICATIONS

(1) Both sides agree in principle on the usefulness of exhibits as an effective means of developing mutual understanding between the peoples of the United States and the Soviet Union. Toward this end both sides will provide for an exchange of exhibits on the peaceful uses of atomic energy in 1958.

(2) Both parties will promote the further development of exchange of publications and various works in the field of science and technology between scientific institutions and societies and between individual scientists and specialists.

(3) Provisions will be made for the Central Scientific Medical Library of the Ministry of Health of the Union of Soviet Socialist Republics and corresponding medical

libraries in the United States to exchange medical journals.

(4) Both parties will promote the exchange of curriculums, textbooks, and scientific pedagogical literature through the appropriate agencies of higher and secondary education and directly between educational institutions.

(5) The Ministry of Health of the Union of Soviet Socialist Republics will arrange to make available in 1958 from 8 to 10 medical films for presentation in the United States. On a reciprocal basis, the United States will arrange to make available the same number of American medical films for presentation in the Soviet Union.

(6) The Ministry of Agriculture of the Union of Soviet Socialist Republics and the Department of Agriculture of the United States are prepared to exchange in 1958 films on such agricultural subjects as stockbreeding, mechanization of agriculture, construction and utilization of irrigation and drainage systems, protection of plants from pests and blights, and fight against erosion.

(7) The representatives of the American and Soviet sides, having exchanged their views on the problems of distributing the magazines Amerika in the Soviet Union and USSR in the United States, have agreed on the desirability and necessity of promoting the distribution of these magazines on the basis of reciprocity. Examination of measures taken by both parties to achieve this end will continue at the ambassadorial level.

SECTION XIV, ESTABLISHMENT OF DIRECT AIR FLIGHTS

Both parties agree in principle to establish on the basis of reciprocity direct air flights between the United States and the Soviet Union. Negotiations on terms and conditions satisfactory to both parties will be conducted by appropriate representatives of each Government at a mutually convenient date to be determined later.

SECTION XV, ENTRY INTO FORCE

The present agreement shall enter into force on the date it is signed.

In witness whereof, the undersigned, duly authorized, have signed the present agreement and have affixed their seals thereto.

Done, in duplicate, in the English and Russian languages, both equally authentic, at Washington this twenty-seventh day of January, one thousand nine hundred fifty-eight.

FOR THE UNITED STATES OF AMERICA:

WILLIAM S. B. LACY [SEAL]

FOR THE UNION OF SOVIET SOCIALIST REPUBLICS:

ZAROUBIN [SEAL]

Part IV HELPING
PEOPLE HELP THEMSELVES

The world-wide demand by people living in the less-developed areas for an improved standard of living has led educators to explore the educational means by which such development might be promoted. The earliest program of education that depended to a large degree upon the willingness of the people at a village level to share in the cost and work was in China, under the leadership of James Yen. Other programs were developed only a little later in Mexico, by Torres Bodet, and in Brazil, by Lourenco Filho.

The two selections that follow are Yen's early description of the program in China and UNESCO suggestions for the elements that make up a Fundamental Education program.

➤➤)⁑《◆

Mass Education in China*

Y. C. JAMES YEN

THE MASS EDUCATION MOVEMENT

I. *The Problem*

"People are the foundation of the nation; if the foundation is firm, then the nation enjoys tranquility," so taught our Chinese ancients several thousand years ago. With how much greater truth is this teaching charged when applied to the Republic of China to-day! To build

* Y. C. James Yen, *The Mass Education Movement in China* (Peking, 1925). [Illustrations and Chinese-character-renderings of words and phrases in the text have been omitted from Yen's document here, but the text has not been edited otherwise.—Ed.]

a firm "foundation" for this Republic or any other republic, one of the great essential needs is the highest possible level of general intelligence of the people.

That China has one fourth of the world's population is a fact familiar to all; but nearly eighty per cent of them do not read or write. Democracy and illiteracy cannot stand side by side. One of the two must go. Which shall it be? China's illiterate masses must be educated and educated soon if democracy is to prove a blessing to herself and to mankind. Hence the Mass Education Movement.

II. *The Policy of the Movement*

1. *Adopting Pai-Hua (Spoken Language)*. One of the chief reasons that account for the overwhelming percentage of illiteracy in China (where learning and scholarship is universally reverenced by high and low alike) is the intricacies of the classical language. For centuries it had been the only recognized literary medium. It is as different from the spoken language as Latin is from English. To learn to use it with any degree of proficiency means a lifetime of study. Thanks to the Literary Revolution of 1917-19, it has succeeded in substituting the Pai-hua for all literary purposes. Not only leading magazines, newspapers, and novels are now published in the Pai-hua, but also standard works on philosophy and sociology. It has practically won its place as the "Kuo Yu," or national language of China to-day. As it is the most widely spoken language in the country and has produced a vast amount of literature in the past, it is the most effective tool in the education of the masses.

2. *Concentrating upon the Illiterates for Whom No Provision Is Made*. According to the latest estimate made by the Chinese National Association for the Advancement of Education, eighty per cent of the Chinese people, or three hundred twenty million, cannot read or write. Out of this total number there are approximately seventy-three million children of school age (between six and twelve) who are not yet in school, and over one hundred million adolescents (between twelve and twenty-

two), not to mention the other one hundred million and more adults. The education of the children of school age has been recognized to be a governmental function and is planned for by the government in its educational system. But what about the two hundred million adolescents and adults who have passed the school age and have been denied a normal chance of schooling? Unless an opportunity is given to them, they will be doomed for life to the terrible "blind alley" of illiteracy and ignorance. It is for the education of these particular groups of illiterates that the Mass Education Movement has sprung up. However, to reach them all in the next decade is clearly impossible. Therefore, it is the policy of the Movement to concentrate principally, though not exclusively, on the education of the one hundred million illiterate adolescents because of their eagerness and ability to learn, and because five to ten years hence they will be the citizens who will play a great part in influencing public opinion and in shaping the destiny of the nation. That the Movement is successful in carrying out this policy is shown by the fact that seventy per cent of the present enrollment of students throughout the country are between twelve and twenty-two years of age.

III. *Methods of Educating the Masses*

The adoption of Pai-hua simplifies immensely the process of learning the written language. But unless the Pai-hua can be so presented to the masses that they can acquire *a maximum of practical vocabulary within a minimum time and at a minimum cost* it would be almost as much beyond the reach of the common man as the classical language was in the past. Reasons for this are obvious: In the first place, the average illiterate man is generally a *busy* man and, having to struggle for his rice, cannot afford four to six years in school. In the second place, the average illiterate man in China is generally a poor man, and unless education is reduced down to his economic level he simply cannot get it. And in the third place, the vocabulary acquired must be practical and useful for him in his daily life as a man and citizen of a Republic.

1. *What to Teach (the "People's Thousand Character Lessons" Based upon the "Foundation Character System")*. The writer had the privilege of serving in the capacity of an educational secretary among the two hundred thousand Chinese laborers in the army "huts" of France during the World War, and of starting the first Pai-hua paper issued in their behalf, known as the *Laborer's Weekly*. This intimate contact with the "coolies" afforded a unique opportunity for the practical study of the problem of mass education. By some years of persistent study and experimentation in China and abroad since the war as a part of the activities of the Educational Department of the National Committee, Y.M.C.A., the *modus operandi* finally developed was the "Foundation Character System" which contains one thousand of the most frequently used characters in Pai-hua. Each character is a jewel which has attained its position among the coveted thousand by fierce competition and by its ability to prove that it can be used in a sufficient number of combinations. This vocabulary was later checked up by the splendid work on "Determination of the Vocabulary of the Common People," directed by Professor H. C. Chen, under the joint auspices of the Chinese National Association for the Advancement of Education and the National Southeastern University, covering a study of Pai-hua literature involving over one million characters. Based upon this foundation vocabulary four readers, called "People's Thousand Character Lessons," were prepared.

This "Foundation Character Course" has been found to meet the above-mentioned requirements of "maximum vocabulary, minimum time, and minimum cost." In the first place, mastery of this course gives the common man a foundation knowledge of Pai-hua and enables him to write simple letters, keep accounts, and read Pai-hua literature intelligently. In the second place, the time required for the completion of the course is only four months of classroom work of an average of one hour each week day, or an average total of ninety-six hours. In the third place, experience in the different campaign centers has shown that each student costs an average of fifty cents (U. S. currency), or one shilling, for the first term and half of that sum every succeeding term.

It ought to be added here that since the publication of the first "People's Thousand Character Lessons" in 1921, a new edition under the capable and joint editorship of Professors W. Tchishin Tao (former dean of the College of Education of National Southeastern University, now general director of the Chinese National Association for the Advancement of Education) and King Chu, formerly of National Peking University, now Chinese editor in chief of the Shanghai Commercial Press) was published in September, 1923. Both Professors Tao and Chu are working voluntarily on the Editorial Board of the National Association of the Mass Education Movement.

2. *How to Teach.* Different methods of teaching have been worked out to meet the varying conditions in different localities. A few of the outstanding ones may be very briefly stated here: (a) The mass method is a scheme of visual instruction and supervised mass recitation using the stereopticon. By this method an experienced teacher can be assigned to a class of two hundred to five hundred students in one room. (b) The individual class method—for a class of twenty to thirty students: in this method textbooks and slates are the material used. (c) The chart method—for a class of forty to sixty students. Practically the same principle of conducting the mass method applies here, but instead of using slides, large-sized paper or cloth charts are used. (d) Reading Circles—for the individuals who cannot attend school at regular hours. A literate in the home or in the neighborhood is asked to be the teacher. The teaching, however, is done under the guidance of an itinerant supervisor who has charge of ten to fifteen homes or shops. (e) People's Question Stations—chiefly for those illiterate people who have no literate member in their family or neighborhood and who are of wandering callings such as

peddlers and ricksha "coolies." These stations are established in shops, families, and organizations, members of which are willing to answer questions on the "People's Thousand Character Lessons."

IV. *Campaign to Reach the People*

It was clearly understood at the outset that in promoting mass education of this kind no spasmodic or individual attempt alone would be of much avail. *Organized* and *coöperative* efforts in the form of a city-wide mass education campaign (so far as the cities are concerned) are essential. Such a campaign aims at enlisting as many *volunteer* workers as possible and coördinating all the forces available in any given community. Each local committee or association, as the case may be, *is entirely responsible for the finance, staff, and equipment of the campaign of its locality.*

In order to get a comprehensive idea of the campaign method, we give here a brief account of a typical city-wide campaign such as has been conducted in many cities.

THE CHEFOO CAMPAIGN

(Chefoo is in the province of Shantung, where China's great sage Confucius was born.)

1. *Organization:* Under the leadership of the local Y.M.C.A., a Mass Education Committee consisting of leading business men, editors, guild leaders, officials, pastors, teachers, and students, was organized. Out of this general committee, five subcommittees on finance, recruiting teachers, recruiting pupils, securing school buildings, and publicity were respectively appointed to set up the campaign.

2. *Publicity.* The Committee used 1,500 posters picturing China's problem of illiteracy and the need for education; 600 official proclamations issued by the Magistrate exhorting all citizens old and young to avail themselves of the opportunity to learn; 20,000 leaflets giving information concerning the "People's Schools"; daily newspaper material. Shops and schools were closed on the day of the opening mass meeting. Over 15,000 people, including business men, students (both men and women), gentry, scholars, and artisans, carry-

ing large banners and lanterns participated in the parade.

3. *Recruiting.* Fifty-two teams of high school boys and girls and college students were organized and sent out to canvass the 52 districts from home to home and shop to shop. In two afternoons the boy teams enrolled 1,466 boys and men, and the girl teams enrolled 633 girls and women. The youngest of those enrolled was seven and the oldest 67 years of age. The great majority, however, were of the adolescent age. One hundred teachers, including gentry, business people, and faculty members of the schools, were enlisted, 70 men and 30 women. These teachers received no salary. An allowance of $4 Mex. per month was given them for ricksha fare. They taught for the regular school term of four months on an average of one hour each week day.

4. *School Buildings.* Fifty buildings were secured in all sections of the city. Primary schools, churches, guild halls, temples, club houses, private residences, police stations, yamens, Y.M.C.A.'s, and Y.W.C.A.'s were all utilized.

5. *The Commencement.* Of the 2,000 students enrolled, over 1,600 attended the classes till the last day. On August 1, 1923, the city celebrated the biggest Commencement in all the history of the province. Mme. Hsiung Hsi-ling, wife of the ex-premier in Yuan Shih-kai's cabinet, presented 1,147 diplomas to the successful students, 775 boys and men, 372 girls and women.

Within the last year and a half Chefoo has celebrated three Commencements with a total number of nearly 4,000 graduates. The slogan of the Chefoo campaign was: "To make Chefoo literate within five years."

V. *The Continuation Education*

Several lines of educational work are being conducted for the graduates, and they are as follows:

1. *Continuation Schools.* After graduation, the students are given an opportunity to go through another four months of schooling in the Continuation Schools where such subjects as civics, geography, history, ele-

mentary science, ethics, and sanitation are taught. In this second period of schooling chief emphasis is laid on *training the students for citizenship*. The Continuation Schools in Chefoo already celebrated their first graduation January 14, 1924.

2. *Scholarships*. Among the graduates of the schools there will doubtless be found a good number who will be worthy of further training in middle schools or even in the colleges and universities. Who dares to say there are no hidden talents and no hidden geniuses among the illiterate millions? The well-to-do among them should be encouraged to go to higher institutions of learning, while the poor but deserving ones should be provided with partial or full scholarships. With the "Scholarship Fund" of the Mass Education Campaign, Chefoo is sending some of its best students to the regular schools of the city.

3. *Literature*. Follow-up literature on various lines, written in simple and attractive style, is of primary importance. In this vitally important task of producing the right kind of literature for the coming millions, the Movement appeals to all literary talents and literary agencies for assistance and coöperation. Books and pamphlets on citizenship, science, sanitation, agriculture, industry, and other literature, like stories, biographies, and songs, have either been published or are being prepared. The Shanghai Commercial Press alone has already published fifty booklets on fifty different subjects.

4. *Reading Clubs*. Reading Clubs are intended chiefly for those graduates who are desirous of furthering their education, but who, for one reason or another, cannot attend the Continuation School. The members meet with their leader, who is generally a literary man or teacher, once or twice a week to hear new terms explained or to participate in the discussion of current events. These clubs, which are also equipped with reading facilities and provided with suitable books and magazines, are situated in centers easily accessible to the graduates in different parts of the locality.

5. *Graduates' Society*. Graduates are organized into what is called "Graduates' Society" (a) for self-improve-

ment and (*b*) for community service. The members meet weekly by section and monthly for the whole city for educational lectures and social functions. For community undertakings, like the Health Campaign and the Anti-opium Campaign, the members of the "Graduates' Society" generally play the leading rôle. What a socializing force they must be in the community as their number increases from year to year!

VI. *Nation-Wide Movement and the National Association*

During the first two years of experimentation, in addition to the Chefoo Campaign described above, two other similar campaigns were conducted in Changsha, Hunan, Central China, and in Hangchow, Chekiang, East China. The results of these experiments proved to be so startling and convincing that the leading educators and social workers of the country began to throw themselves into the Movement with boundless enthusiasm for a nation-wide campaign. The outstanding leaders among them were Mme. Hsiung hsi-ling, wife of the ex-premier and a well-known social reformer, Professor W. Tchishin Tao, general director of the Chinese National Association for the Advancement of Education, President P. C. Wang, of the Law College of the province of Kiangsu, and Professor King Chu, formerly of National Peking University. Within one year the provinces, one after another, began to recruit students by the thousand. According to the reports of the sales agencies of the Movement, over two million textbooks have been sold. Those who are acquainted with the social habits of the Chinese in loaning and sharing books among relatives and friends can well imagine the actual number of students using these books.

With the nation-wide spread of the work, the leaders of the Movement felt that a central organization to give general supervision and systematic promotion was urgently needed. So, under the leadership of Mme. Hsiung Hsi-ling, Drs. Yuan Hsi-tao, former Vice Minister of Education, P. W. Kuo, president of National Southeastern

University, W. Tchishin Tao, Huh Suh, leader of the Renaissance Movement, Huang Yenpai, president of the National Vocational Association, and Chang Po-ling, president of Nankai University, and with the coöperation of the Chinese National Association for the Advancement of Education, a National Convention on Mass Education was called in Tsing Hua College, Peking, August, 1923. In this representative gathering from twenty provinces the National Association of the Mass Education Movement was organized with an Executive Board of nine Directors and a National Board of Directors composed of two representatives from each province. Mme. Hsiung hsi-ling was elected unanimously the chairman of the Board and concurrently of the National Association.

Since the inauguration of the National Association, thirty-two city *self-supporting* Mass Education Associations have sprung up in strategic centers like Wuchang, Changsha, Anking, Nanchang, Nanking, Peking, Tientsin, Shanghai, Hangchow, Canton, Chengtu, Kirin, and Harbin. The following is a brief account of a typical Mass Education Association.

The Nanking Mass Education Association. The Nanking Mass Education Association was organized with a Board of Directors representing various interests of the community with Dr. Yuan Hsi-tao as chairman and Mr. Yen Meng-fan, the provincial treasurer, as the treasurer. The secretarial staff, which is composed of allocated men and women from leading educational and social institutions of Nanking, is under the general secretaryship of Professor P. C. Wang, president of Kiangsu Law College and an active social worker. A part of General Li's Memorial Buildings in the East City is given over as the headquarters of the Association; Marshal Chieh Hsiyuan, its honorary chairman, gave $10,000 to the Association. There are altogether in the city 126 schools, with a total enrollment of over five thousand students.

The first group of the five thousand students enrolled had their first graduation on the twenty-second of December, 1923, in the Public Recreation Ground. Governor Han Tsz-shih, one of the strong supporters of the Mass Education Movement, spoke at the Commencement and gave out 602 diplomas. Over six thousand people attended. Since then, Nanking has graduated three different groups totaling over three thousand graduates. The *Commoner,* issued by the Association for the graduates based upon the Thousand Character vocabulary and the *Mass Education Forum,* issued weekly for the teachers and promoters of the Movement and the general public, are already enjoying a wide circulation in the country.

VII. *Army Education*

It can be readily understood that the army makes an ideal place for the establishment of a system of compulsory education. And with the men living together in large numbers, the "mass method" of teaching as mentioned in a preceding paragraph, could be applied most effectively.

China has an illiterate as well as a big army. For this reason, the Mass Education Movement has been trying to make its way into the army. Through the progressive leadership of General Chang Hsieh-liang, son of Marshal Chang Tso-ling of Manchuria, the first experiment of army education was made in Mukden. The organization for the work consisted of a general committee of three generals and four colonels headed by General Chang himself. Three committees were appointed: the Editorial Committee to deal with literature and textbooks, the Educational Committee to give supervision and study method of teaching, and the Business Committee to take charge of finance and supplies. For equipment of the work, fifty thousand textbooks and sixty stereopticons with five thousand colored slides were used.

A training school was conducted for one week for three hundred officers. A survey was made of the degree of illiteracy and and it was discovered that on the average only twenty-five out of each battalion of one hundred fifty could read and write. So the other one hundred twenty-five in the battalion formed a convenient class unit for the "mass method." With each battalion class an officer teacher was intrusted to take up the first half of the daily school period with instruction by means of the stereopticon and picture and character slides. During the second half of the period the class is divided into sections consisting of fifteen to twenty each for purposes of personal supervision by assistant teachers. During the non-class hours each section of the soldier-pupils received additional help from what was called the "Guide," who was held responsible for answering questions on the pronunciation and meaning of the characters in the text. These two groups (assistants and guides) were taken from the twenty-five literate men in each battalion. The whole system was so arranged that every officer and private in the army worked: some learning, some teaching, and some assisting. One of its by-products was the fostering of the spirit of comradeship and morale in the army.

Upon the completion of the first book of the "People's Thousand Character Lessons" the Editorial Committee of the Mukden Army issued a *Soldier's Weekly,* based upon the vocabulary of the first book and illustrated with pictures. The editors were greatly surprised to find that a variety of subjects could be touched upon with just two hundred fifty "Foundation Characters." Tracts and booklets of special interest to the soldier limited to the Thousand Character vocabulary were issued by the Editorial Committee from time to time. As a preliminary step towards the formulation of a continuation program, a scientific study was made of the "soldier's vocabulary" by the Editorial and Educational committees with a view to working out a course which would be adapted to the education of the army.

The results of the first two months of work were nothing short of miraculous. But, unfortunately, hostilities broke out between Mukden and Peking and consequently all educational activities had to be stopped. Short-lived as this campaign was it exerted a far-reaching influence all over the country. In fact just before the outbreak of the war in question, several generals had already sent in requests to have mass education conducted in their respective armies. As long as there is little hope of disbanding the troops, the only attitude for an educational movement such as ours to take is the *positive* attitude, that is, instead of standing aloof or ceaselessly condemning, it should go into the army and to educate it. There is no doubt that through the mass education program the Movement has a unique opportunity of helping to turn the present "army peril" into positive good for the upbuilding of China.

VIII. *Rural Education*

Undoubtedly the greater battle of the Mass Education Movement against illiteracy will have to be fought not so much in the towns, as in the villages, where nearly three fourths of China's illiterate millions live. However, if the village is to be conquered, the town must first be won. The village itself can do little without the leadership of the town. The Movement, which has so far concentrated its attack principally upon the cities, has, of course, not yet won its battle in the town; but it has succeeded, through the concrete results achieved in the provinces, in winning the confidence of the public, and in quickening the conscience and stirring the imagination of the members the "upper classes," thousands of whom give money and service freely for the advancement of its cause. Having thus established itself in the cities, the Movement is in a favorable position both to interest men to work in the rural field, where life is hard and unattractive, and also to enlist the coöperation of other educational and social institutions.

1. *General Plan.* The general plan of the Movement is to select one or two typical rural districts in north, south, east, west, and central China, respectively, for intensive and extensive experimentations. By "intensive experiment" is meant that the work be concentrated in a chosen area until (1) illiteracy is wiped out, (2) sanitary measures introduced, and (3) general farming reforms effected. In other words, the Movement aims, in coöperation with other educational, social, and religious institutions, to make it a model district in education and in

general social and economic improvement, so that it may be used as a demonstration and training center for other districts. While intensive experiments of this kind are being undertaken in the chosen areas, the Movement promotes its program extensively to as many villages as possible and as rapidly as possible.

2. *Experiments as Conducted in North China*. During the last troublous year, in spite of war and rumors of war, a fair beginning has been made along "extensive" lines in two areas in North China. The following is a brief account.

a. *Paoting Area*. Paoting is located in the province of Chihli. In this Paoting area, which used to be a "fu," or prefecture, during the Manchu régime, there are about twenty "hsiens," or districts, with an average of three hundred villages each. In conducting this experiment here, the rural workers of the American Board Mission, both Chinese and foreign, are giving the movement the best of coöperation. Within a period of four months some five thousand students, male and female, ranging from twelve to forty-five years of age, have been enrolled in the People's Schools of about two hundred villages, covering a territory of twelve "hsiens." A two-day training conference was conducted in the head district, Paoting, for the teachers and workers of the whole area.

The first groups of students enrolled had already celebrated their respective villages. The director of the Department of Rural Education of our National Association attended several of the village commencements and distributed the "Diplomas of Literate Citizen" to the village graduate which were all stamped with the official seal of the magistrate. It was most encouraging to learn, upon the return of the director, that the school which received the highest prizes in one whole "hsien," was the school taught by a man who learned his text in a neighboring village in the morning and taught it in the evening.

The results of the work has had far-reaching influence, for the most recent report from the Paoting area shows that the magistrates of the neighboring "hsiens" have, entirely on their own initiative, started another one hundred or more People's Schools and with an additional enrollment of nearly five thousand students. At the urgent request of the field workers and teachers the Department of Rural Education is publishing a weekly paper called the *Farmer,* for the graduates of the villages.

b. Chinchao, or the Peking Metropolitan Area. Under the capable and conscientious leadership of the governor of the Peking metropolitan area, Mr. Shueh Tsz-liang, a very significant rural experiment is being conducted in Chinchao. It has twenty "hsiens" under its jurisdiction, varying from one hundred to one thousand villages each. In promoting this rural program, Governor Shueh broke the usual "official rule" of merely issuing orders and proclamations. He believed in the principle of "charity at home first," so he started mass education first at his own *yamen.* Not only *all* the employees must attend the classes but also the female members of their families, wives and daughters. There are now four People's Schools, two for men and two for women, going on every evening in the yamen. Early next June, these employees are expected to receive their "Diplomas of Literate Citizen" from the governor himself.

While the work in the yamen was in progress, Governor Shueh called together all the magistrates of the twenty "hsiens" to attend a Mass Education Training Conference as well as to discuss ways and means of extending the program of Mass Education to the whole of Chinchao. The final plan, as worked out by the Conference, was to make mass education compulsory throughout the metropolitan area. To carry this out the program is divided into three educational periods. It is calculated that by the end of the third period, which is about February, 1927, all the illiterate adolescents, male and female (between twelve and twenty-two years of age) will have been taken into the "People's Schools." The program of the first period is at present in operation in all the "hsiens." A few of them have already entered into the second period. Being the first metropolitan area of the capital of China, this Chinchao experiment is of great significance, and will in the near future exert tremendous influence throughout the county in rural mass education.

Comparing the work conducted in the village with that in the city, one finds that the conditions in the former are even more favorable for mass education than those in the latter. In the first place, the village folk have been very sadly neglected and consequently appreciate every little worth-while thing done on their behalf and this makes them much more teachable and earnest than the town people. Secondly, unlike the city, there are scarcely any attractions or detractions in the village and the students are therefore more faithful and regular in their school attendance. Thirdly, being a small community of families, where everybody knows practically everybody else in the village, there prevails among them a strong family spirit or community consciousness, which one finds generally weak or totally lacking in cities, and which is essential for the successful promotion of the work. Fourthly, in North China, there are four to six idle months in fall and winter, and most of the farming people can attend from four to six hours a day. Lastly, but not least, Chinese country folks are among the most industrious and hard-working of the entire people. For these if for no other reasons the illiterate farmer has at least as good a chance in getting an education as his town cousin. Morally, economically as well as numerically, China's backbone is her rural people, and therefore the promotion of rural education is of paramount and fundamental importance.

IX. *The Significance of the Movement*

The full significance of the Movement will, of course, not be seen until a decade or more later. However, there are a few distinct contributions of "by-products" of great value that may be briefly touched upon here:

1. *The First Organized Attempt on a Large Scale to Educate the Masses.* While China has always given first place to education, and acquiring of the best education

possible was open to all from the coolie to the prince, there has never been any *organized* attempt made to bring education to the masses. Reading has been traditionally looked upon by the people as a specialty to be pursued exclusively by the scholar. There has been, in reality, what is called the "aristocracy of learning." This Movement, in championing the cause of "education for all," and in working systematically and persistently to bring education within the reach of all, bids fair to revolutionize the thought life of the masses.

2. *A Movement of the People, by the People, and for the People*. It is a Movement *of* the people. In all the campaign centers and associations the committee members or those of the Board of Directors are, without exception, composed of the representative members of the community, like business, education, industry, and labor. It is a Movement *by* the people. The promotion of the campaign, and the teaching and supervision of the schools are done voluntarily by the public-spirited members of the community, such as business men, gentry, pastors, teachers, and students of the schools and colleges. The campaign fund is also contributed by the well-to-do members of the community from all classes. And it is a Movement *for* the people. It sets out definitely to enlist the service and coöperation of the educated and the well-to-do to uplift the illiterate members of the community.

3. *A Stimulus to More Adequate Education*. One of the inevitable results of the work of the Mass Education Movement is the boosting of education wherever it goes. On the one hand, it arouses the public sentiment of the leaders for general educational reform, and on the other hand, it creates a desire on the part of rank and file for more adequate education. It need not take a great mind to imagine what effect it must have upon a community when it turns out literates by the thousands each year. Further, it is quite obvious that in giving education to the illiterate grown-ups the Movement is not only helping to save the present generation from illiteracy and ignorance but also indirectly the next generation. The simple reason is that when the fathers and mothers, elder

brothers and sisters, are educated, the younger generation will surely stand a better chance of getting an education.

4. *Towards the Making of a New Literature.* Graduates from the "People's Schools" are turning out in great
numbers each year. The demand for literature is daily
increasing. The Movement cannot, of course, be expected
to produce all the literature to meet the needs of the
coming reading population; but it is trying to, through
its own publications, set a right standard for the country
and also stimulate other institutions and individuals to
get out literature for the common people. Hitherto, almost anything worth while done in writing had been
done for the scholar and practically nothing for the common people. It is most encouraging to see, however, that
national educational institutions, like the National
Southeastern University, the Chinese National Association for the Advancement of Education, the National
Committee, the Y. M. C. A., and commercial publishing
houses, like the Shanghai Commercial Press and the
Chung Hwa Book Company, are making extensive plans
to publish literature to meet the demands of the ever-
increasing reading population. *A "people's literature" is
in the making.* That the leading scholars of the nation
are actively interested in this project is proved by the
fact that men like Dr. Hu Suh, leader of the Renaissance
movement, Professor Chien Hsuen-tung, a novelist of
nation-wide renown, Dr. Hsiung Hsi-ling, the ex-premier,
Professor Lin Tu-ting, are serving on the "National
Council on People's Literature of the Mass Education
Movement."

5. *Training for True Citizenship.* One of the greatest
weaknesses in Chinese life is the lack of coöperative action. China has been compared to a "dish of scattered
sand"! There is hardly a greater need in a community
than to have training in a *common* task in which every
one believes and in which all can unite their efforts. To
the Chinese mind the appeal of education is irresistible,
which is undoubtedly the result of four thousand years
of civilization. The mass education program provides

favorable conditions for united effort where no material gain is possible, and where unselfish service is demanded. Furthermore, by participating in this program the well-to-do and the educated members come to the realization that the welfare of the community depends upon the development and the intelligence of the masses. In the meantime, as these illiterate people themselves are given this opportunity for self-development, it creates in them a sense of personal worth as well as a sense of responsibility in the life of the community and the nation.

6. *The Unification of the Nation.* It is true that "North" and "South" are at odds with each other. Yet "North" and "South" are coöperating in the movement. Chihli, Kwangtung, Fengtien, Szechwan, Hupeh, and Yünnan are all working for the *common* cause, "A Literate China." True, *politically,* China is divided, but in education and particularly in mass education, she is one. Thus through a common effort to advance a common cause such as that championed by the Mass Education Movement, China can be molded into one united nation.

7. *Towards the Realization of World Peace.* The world can ill afford to see China's millions kept ignorant and ignored. Surely with her immense man power, her vast natural and mineral resources, and her four thousand years of civilization she must have something to contribute to the peace and progress of the world. Her people are a peace-loving people. Such time-honored teachings as "All under heaven, one Family" and "All races, one Body" are only typical of the writings and philosophies of her sages and great teachers. Indeed, the sooner China's illiterate masses are educated, the sooner will the world have the added moral force as well as the material assistance of four hundred million intelligent, peace-loving people to help to hasten the day of universal peace and brotherhood among mankind.

The Elements of Fundamental Education*

When one turns to practical examples of fundamental education work, one is struck by the wide variety of content, methods and even of immediate aims. This is natural. The special problems which each project must face, the national culture and local traditions which it seeks to develop and enrich, the physical environment in which the people concerned must live and work and the resources of money and trained personnel available will all influence the nature and direction of its development.

However, it is possible to examine more closely the various elements that go to make fundamental education. This is done in the following pages; not with the intention of proposing a standardized pattern, but only in the hope that governments, organizations and individuals responsible for national campaigns or local projects may find ideas which they may adapt to their particular needs. It should not be assumed that all the elements here discussed are to be found in any single programme, still less in any one local project. This section gives only a brief indication of points later discussed in detail.

The analysis starts with the schools. The provision of universal, free and compulsory primary education is an ideal which must be set for any fundamental education programme; it cannot be claimed that the essential minimum fundamental education has been provided until all children have the opportunity to obtain a sound elementary schooling. Even before such a goal is reached the schools can contribute a great deal to the life of the community. But these facts do not mean that the mere numerical increase of schools is the first, or necessarily the most important, aim. Quality—in terms of local needs —should be considered before quantity.

* UNESCO, *Fundamental Education* (Paris, UNESCO, 1949), pp. 14-17.

Fundamental education aims at reaching all sections of the community, children and adults, women as well as men. It is generally found that children soon lose the benefits they derive from a few years of schooling if they are re-absorbed into an illiterate and apathetic community. There is clearly a close connexion between child and adult education. Where little or no formal schooling exists, the programme may first be directed in an informal and practical way towards the adults. The techniques of adult education (which differ considerably from those found in schools) are used both to make the community aware of its problems and to bring forward the natural leaders; and as the incentives for improvement develop the programme should provide the people with opportunities for learning the knowledge and skills that make improvement possible.

Among adults, work with women has special importance because they all too often have an inferior status which can be remedied through education, and also because of their influence in the home and in the early life of the children.

The most pressing needs and problems of each community represent the starting point for the fundamental education programme. Where, for instance, endemic diseases are undermining the vitality of the people, a community health campaign, in which health education is linked with curative medicine and sanitary engineering, may take precedence even over the construction of the first school.

The example of a health campaign is a particular one. In general, the pattern of fundamental education is most clearly seen in relation to the vast rural areas of the world. The peasant or tribal peoples who provide the world with all-important primary products are engaged in a ceaseless struggle with their physical environment. They are often constrained by the prevailing social and economic system and usually lack the scientific knowledge and the skills which would give them access to a fuller and more productive life. Here fundamental education is an important means for agricultural improvement and the betterment of social conditions. If, further, it can help to counteract the wastage of natural resources caused by improvident agriculture and erosion, it will contribute also to world prosperity and peace.

The need for a minimum fundamental education is equally evident among the under-privileged inhabitants of industrial towns and cities. Here the chief activity may be literacy campaigns and 'night classes'—remedial education—or group activities which provide opportunities for the better use of leisure or which bring the school more actively into the life of the people. In urban areas there are usually a number of social welfare and adult education agencies, all of which carry out programmes of fundamental education; the problem may be one of co-ordination of work rather than of initiation.

Fundamental education is designed to 'help people to achieve the social and economic progress which will enable them to take their place in the modern world.' But low living standards cannot be raised by educational means alone. Education must be integrated with economic development schemes, including, in certain circumstances, the development of local industries. Such work aims at better use of the resources that are locally available, and co-operatives may provide the framework to ensure that the people themselves control the means of improvement. The connexion between fundamental education and standard of living is a very close one; for education in skills and techniques, and in the principles of co-operation, are indispensable to economic progress; and at the same time only a rising standard of living can give meaning or permanence to educational work.

Areas where a high proportion of the people are illiterate are the main field for fundamental education. The skills of reading, writing and counting are not, however, an end in themselves. Rather they are the essential means to the achievement of a fuller and more creative life. Where the incentive to read and write is already present, a fundamental education programme may find its point of attack through a literacy campaign, using the simple texts as a means of teaching other knowledge and attitudes. Where no incentive to literacy exists it is a function of fundamental education first to stimulate, and then to satisfy, the demand for it.

A multiplicity of local languages or dialects may present special problems; at times the only solution seems to be to teach a second or auxiliary language, important enough to carry a literature of its own.

The written word is the most obvious medium for education, but it also has shortcomings. All available techniques—such as discussion and demonstration—and the modern audio-visual media, the film, filmstrip and radio, should be used in order to present information and ideas more vividly. Where the majority of the people cannot read, such media acquire a special value. Museum and library techniques need also to be adapted to serve illiterate and newly literate peoples; when so adapted, they take an important place in the programme.

The analysis thus far has dealt mainly with material improvement; but if fundamental education is to 'help people to develop what is best in their own culture' the whole purpose and method of education must be interpreted afresh. Local culture consists, in part, of traditional modes of self-expression, and these must find a place in the programme. But more important is the receptive and sympathetic approach which is demanded of the educator. People who are technologically backward may possess personal qualities, values and traditions of a higher order than those found among more industrialized groups. Progress, at best, is a relative term. There is no place in fundamental education for the view that illiterate people are children who should be disciplined into progress either by force or by the cut-and-dried plans of well-intentioned outsiders. The purpose of all fundamental education work is to obtain the active participation of the people themselves in shaping their own future. This may seem slow, but only on a foundation of popular assent and understanding can lasting progress be made.

Fundamental education should always fit into the framework of the existing educational system, local or national. Secondary, university and higher technical education are not fundamental education, but they are essential to it. Such institutions provide the community with its leaders, teachers and extension workers, and in doing so give the more aspiring members of the community the means for leading a fuller, useful life.

The central principle in fundamental education is that of integration. The aim implied above is to enable the individual to adjust satisfactorily to his social and physical environment; and to achieve this, the fundamental education programme has to be integrated with education at other levels and with economic development and social services.

Part V COMMUNICATION

-»»×«‹-

International Communication
and the World Society*

ROBERT C. ANGELL

Rapid long-range transportation now brings face to face many people from widely distant and different parts of the world; yet a few decades ago most people rarely traveled beyond the borders of their own countries. Coupled with the rapid development of transportation has been the extension of mass communication throughout the world. Inaccessible desert and mountain communities are now reached by radio. The Indians of the mountains of Colombia can now discuss international affairs with the nomads of the Middle East. Mass literacy campaigns have produced a demand for reading materials for the newly literate. The production of inexpensive books has made available to millions materials that were too expensive a few years ago.

In his essay, Robert C. Angell examines the relationship of international communication to the world society.

My task is, I take it, to scrutinize the far-flung process of international communication with a view to determining whether or not it is contributing, or may contribute, to the growth of consensus among the peoples of the world. Implicit in such a statement of the task is a definition of communication that is at variance with the word's original meaning—to make things common. We

* Reprinted from *The World Community*, edited by Quincy Wright (1948), pp. 145ff., by permission of the publisher. (Copyright 1948, by The University of Chicago Press.)

shall here mean by it merely the passing of ideas from one mind to another. The receiving mind may not accept the ideas, and even the originating mind may not believe them. One further explanation should be made. I have not dealt with communication that takes place within the boundaries of one nation but which refers to the people of another nation, though admitting its great importance. It seems to me that the inclusion of this in the scope of international communication would so broaden the problem as to rob this paper of all unity of conception and treatment.

I shall hardly touch upon the movement of people from country to country. This, of course, is actually one form of communication. During the war it was a very important one, because large numbers of men spent long periods away from home among strangers. But in peacetime the bulk of contacts of this kind are made by two groups of persons: businessmen and tourists. The contacts in both cases are fleeting and segmental. Since the visitors from abroad do not stay long enough to settle down into a life-routine, they frequently show all the instability and impulsiveness that sociologists characterize as *anomie*. They neither make friends with natives nor win their admiration. Exchange of students and professors is a different matter. Long residence and involvement in a way of life shared by natives produce real fellowship. But such exchange goes on in such small measure at present as to be a very minor factor in the general situation.

Though most of us undoubtedly believe that the volume of international communication is increasing year by year, we cannot assume that to be the case. The difficulties of measuring the volume of communication across national borders are, however, very great. For some media we can obtain statistics; for others, we cannot. The discussion will proceed in terms of six channels of communication under two main heads. Point-to-point communication includes mail, on the one hand, and cable and radiotelegraph messages, on the other. International telephone traffic is not large enough to be significant. Under mass communication I will include wire and wireless press dispatches, short-wave broadcasting, moving pictures, and magazines and books. Most of the trends that I will give are for the United States alone. It seemed impossible to assemble world-wide data at this time. I do not make the assumption that the trends for the United States are typical of the world, but I do assume that we know enough about the peculiar position of the United States in the world to be able to make rough corrections and thus arrive at some conception of global trends.

The figures on foreign mail for selected years show very clearly that point-to-point communication of this type is closely related to the movement of persons. It is evident that immigrants into a country continue to write relatives and friends in the homeland for years after their migration. But, as the tide of immigration slows up and then ceases, as happened about 1930, there is a direct reflection of this process in the dispatch of foreign mail. Just before the recent war it is evident that the lessening number of immigrant letters was being offset by a rising trend, probably in commercial correspondence. The peak war figure (1945) again shows the importance of the movement of persons, this time members of our armed services; and the decline in 1946 reflects their return home in large numbers. Whether these men made friendships abroad that will keep our mail communication higher than it was before the war for some time to come is an interesting question to which we cannot give an answer.

Since mail communication is so closely tied to migration, the world trends in mail communication may be estimated from a consideration of population movements around the globe. The declining birth rates in Europe in the twentieth century have slowed down the outward movement of population that was so marked until World War I. The flight of refugees before Hitler and the forced movements of peoples incident to the war and its aftermath are not likely to give rise to extensive mail communication for the simple reason that those who have migrated have left few of their own kind behind. In other parts of the world I am not aware that there has been any sharp variation in trends. My conclusion would therefore be that person-to-person mail communication throughout the world is declining somewhat but that this is offset in part by increasing business correspondence.

No one series of data can give the picture with respect to cable and wireless or radiotelegraph communication for the United States because of the differing ways in which the data have been gathered. There can be no doubt that, so far as the United States is concerned, there is a constantly increasing flow of messages of this kind to and from the remainder of the world. And there is no reason to suppose that we are unrepresentative of the global situation in this regard. Because we industrialized earlier than most parts of the world, it can be argued that the trend of recent decades in the United States understates rather than overstates the world trend.

From a consideration of the data so far adduced it would appear that the decline in mail communication is probably not being offset by the increase in cable and radiotelegraph communication. Though the latter was growing rapidly just before World War II, only about one two-hundredth as many words were being transmitted this way as by mail (assuming the average letter to contain three hundred words). In the absence of counter-evidence, we must assume that the world will tend to revert to something like this pre-war situation.

Point-to-point communication is, however, probably going to be only a minor factor in the development of the world society. Although sociologists are impressed by the superiority for purposes of social integration of the intimate type of communication that is represented by personal letters, it is obviously the mass agencies of communication that, because of their tremendous reach, hold the greatest hope for world understanding.

The best index I have been able to discover of international newspaper communication is the foreign press traffic transmitted by American companies engaged in the cable and radiotelegraph businesses. These figures show a great increase from the period of the twenties to the period of the late thirties and early forties. There can be not the slightest doubt that, so far as the world situation is reflected by press messages to and from the United States, newspapers have been constantly improving their foreign coverage. Though our press is undoubtedly able to afford greater coverage than the press of other nations, there is no reason to suppose that the trend shown is not a world-wide one.

International short-wave broadcasting was developed in the thirties by European countries and by Japan. Before Pearl Harbor the United States did very little in this field. There were then seven "licensees" operating transmitters, a few hours a week, but only one of them had been able to obtain a subsidy sufficient to cover costs.[1] All this changed very rapidly with our entry into the war. We soon caught up with the European countries, and ultimately we surpassed them. The war peak was reached in 1944. The Russians were then beaming more than 90 hours of broadcasting a day in 37 languages through 15 short-wave transmitters.[2] In the same year Great Britain was transmitting almost 110 hours a day in 39 languages, and the United States more than 153 hours in 34 languages.[3] All three have reduced these schedules considerably since the war but are still maintaining a level infinitely higher than before the war. Russia is now operating short-wave transmitters 42 hours a day in 30 languages, the British Broadcasting Corporation, 88 hours in 46 languages, and "The Voice of the U.S.A.," 57 hours in 25 languages over 36 transmitters.[4] Our broadcasts are sponsored by the Office of International Information and Cultural Affairs of the State Department. At the moment it appears certain that Congress will greatly reduce our national effort in this field.

1 Llewellyn White and Robert D. Leigh, *Peoples Speaking to Peoples* (1946), p. 43.

2 *New York Times*, April 27, 1947.

3 *Education on the Air: 16th Yearbook of the Institute for Education by Radio*, 1945, p. 40.

4 *New York Times*, April 27, 1947.

I have been unable to obtain statistical data on the international exchange of films. Until the early thirties it seems clear that almost all traffic was outward from the United States and that the foreign market was very profitable to Hollywood. With the advent of the sound picture, language barriers became more important. The competition between American and foreign films became keener outside the United States. British films were the only ones that could invade the American market. In the late thirties somewhat more than two hundred foreign-produced films were shown in this country yearly,[5] while between 35 and 40 per cent of the world revenue for film rentals was received from outside the United States by American distributors.[6] At the present time foreign nations are trying to build up their own moving-picture industries and are forcing their own exhibitors to keep a certain ratio between domestic films and the importations from Hollywood.

Although magazines and books are not such pervasive agencies of mass communication as the newspaper, the radio, and the moving picture, they cannot be ignored. It makes little difference whether such printed matter is in the original language or translated, whether shipped abroad or produced abroad. The main point is that the indigenous culture of one country is communicated to another. World interchange of books has been going on for centuries. There is every reason to believe that there has been a steady acceleration of the process. Although American book publishers have sold a very small percentage of their product abroad, many pirated editions in other languages have been issued. European publishers have been far ahead of ours in cultivating foreign markets. With respect to magazines, on the other hand, we have been the most successful. *Reader's Digest* publishes seven foreign-language editions, and *Time* and *Newsweek* publish English editions in foreign countries. It is said that in a few parts of the world *Reader's Digest*

5 See *President's Annual Report to the Motion Picture Producers and Distributors of America,* various years.

6 *Ibid.,* March 30, 1942. p. 53.

outcirculates any domestic magazine. Because of the expense of magazines and books, several countries including our own have set up library and reading-room facilities in large cities abroad. We have seventy-five of these in forty-five foreign countries, and it is estimated that they serve three and one-half million readers a year.[7] This seems to indicate that there are large numbers of persons abroad to which every nation can cater by supplying them with accurate information about its own people and with representative examples of their creative writing.

The immediate future may see some important changes in the amount of international mass communication. Radiotelegraph, which is fast replacing cables, is likely to be used increasingly for multiple-address broadcasting. Britain and Russia are showing the way in this field. By this technique news can be beamed to all the press-receiving stations over a wide area in a single transmission. It is now mechanically possible for any publication in the world to receive 100,000 words of foreign news daily. With respect to short-wave radio, we may expect that other European countries and the oriental nations will enter the field in competition with Russia, Britain, the United States, and France. If we drastically cut down our efforts of this kind, we shall be taking a course that others probably will not follow. In the field of motion pictures, the future may not see a greater number of films crossing national borders, but the chances are that there will be more exchange among nations and less domination by Hollywood. There will be more interaction. Probably the same may be said for magazines and books. Our book-publishing industry awakened to our backwardness in cultivating foreign markets and for a time operated the United States International Book Association. It is likely that the success of our magazines in invading foreign territory will stimulate competition from other nations. There is also a real likelihood that truly international magazines will emerge, drawing on con-

[7] Ferdinand Kuhn, "Letting the Whole World Know," *Survey Graphic*, XXXV (December, 1946), 493.

tributors from all over the world, and publishing in different languages.

Thus far we have been concerned merely with the amount of communication flowing from one nation to another. But quantity is not nearly so important as quality or content. If most of what is passing back and forth is on subjects unimportant for international good will, or if it is warped to the degree that no good purpose is served by its transmission, then quantity is of no significance whatever. Before one can deal with the crucial question of quality, it seems necessary to formulate a theory of international communication. If our aim is to achieve peace among nations, we should ask ourselves what, under existing conditions, are the essential functions of such communication.

It seems to me that the basic need is to communicate the way of life of different peoples to one another so as to achieve three objectives: (1) an appreciation of the common human qualities underlying cultural differences; (2) an understanding of the central values of other cultures; and (3) a realization that the different value systems of the world's peoples are each compatible with the universal human qualities even when not compatible with each other. The achievement of these three objectives would not insure world peace, since many of us who understood how the Nazis got that way still felt we had to go to war with them. But appreciation of the fact that the different cultures have at least a common basis in human nature (and many pairs of cultures have more than that) would give all peoples more tolerance toward one another and more hope that incompatible value systems could gradually be modified.

*   *   *

"The Family of Man" *

MARTIN S. DWORKIN

In the following essay Martin S. Dworkin comments on the use of photography as a means of international communication, using Edward Steichen's exhibition, "The Family of Man," as an outstanding example.

No exhibition of photographs has received the interest and acclaim accorded 'The Family of Man', conceived and created by Edward Steichen—himself one of the greatest photographers—with the assistance of Wayne Miller. At New York's Museum of Modern Art, where Steichen is director of the department of photography, the exhibition attracted more than a quarter of a million visitors during its three-month stay early in 1955. The response grew enormously on its tour of the United States of America. In Minneapolis, Dallas, Cleveland, Philadelphia, Baltimore, and Pittsburgh, larger crowds than had ever attended museum exhibitions were counted. As the full-size edition continued traveling during 1957 and 1958, to Los Angeles, San Francisco, Toronto (Canada), and other cities, several smaller versions were also circulated, reaching unnumbered people who thereby had their first experience of formally presented art.

In Europe and Asia, 'The Family of Man', presented under the auspices of the United States Information Agency, impressed new multitudes—both as the most ambitious use of photographs hitherto attempted, and by its

* *Fundamental and Adult Education*, Vol. X, 1958, No. 4, pp. 177-180. This essay is based on an article originally published in *The Progressive Magazine* and is used with the author's permission.

theme of the inherent community of mankind. In addition to first-hand impact upon viewers, the exhibition
has exerted incalculable influence in publications
throughout the world, which carried accounts and com-
mentaries, often considerably illustrated. A book containing all the pictures and thematic texts has, in fact,
become one of the most successful illustrated volumes
ever published.

That a collection of photographs could excite such a
response has been judged an absolute proof of the vitality
of photography as a medium of artistic expression and
communication. Some critics and photographers have
been dubious about the theme or organic concept—and
also about Steichen's selection of photographs and way
of ordering them into a unitary whole. But 'The Family
of Man' has been nothing if not popular. The public apparently understands the concept, and likes it, while enjoying the experience of looking at a large number of
photographs carefully arranged in a museum or exhibition hall.

In fact, the greatest importance of 'The Family of
Man' lies in this understanding, or successful communication of ideas—evidence of the coming to maturity of
a language and the refinement of means of using it. Nobody is puzzled about the theme, and no critic com-
plains about recondite meanings. If Steichen's philosophy
of man is essentially fuzzy, and the show relentlessly
sentimental in consequence, this is all eminently clear.
What is not understood is *why* it is all so clear. The
space of museums has been used to present 503 photographs from 68 countries, organized deliberately to
convey a particular message—and it has worked. If
this seems unremarkable, it is only because we have
learned so much so well—albeit in a time so amazingly
short that people still young may recall its beginning.

Steichen has been the leader in experimenting with
the form of the photographic exhibition as a vehicle for
ideas. His earlier shows: 'In and Out of Focus', 'The
Exact Instant', and particularly 'The Korean War', pic-
torially illuminated specific themes. 'The Family of Man'

articulates a generalized philosophy. The photographs are arranged in groups, and presented around lyrical epigrams or proverbs out of many cultures: Homer, Lao-tze, Shakespeare, Deuteronomy, Einstein, Montaigne, the Kwakiutl Indians, James Joyce, Genesis, the Pueblos, the Bhagavad-Gita, the Charter of the United Nations. The prevailing temper is joyous, rhapsodic—represented by Eugene Harris's repeated *leit-motiv* picture of a happy Andean piper boy. Each group subtheme advances the observer along the general argument of the exhibition, expressed in a prologue by Carl Sandburg—who is by happy co-incidence Steichen's brother-in-law. Man, it is declared, belongs to a single family, whatever his culture, or colour, or nation, or particular circumstances.

The pictures take this up at once. Man everywhere is equally naked in nature—symbolized by Wynn Bullock's striking photograph of a nude child asleep in a forest glade, embedded in new leaves and surrounded by primeval ferns. Man loves, he weds, he begets children, tenderly treated—who grow, and play, and show those fears and angers that presage adult conflicts. He works, and his labour in the earth nourishes him; he sings and dances, laughs and celebrates, studies and ponders, courts and converses, dies and mourns and marks his passing. But life flows on, and there is agony, hunger, misery—and dreams of hope, humility, and reverence for deity.

People are fundamentally good and kind; but they struggle, they need justice from themselves, the mutual concern of self-government. For a soldier's corpse in a blasted earth, there is Sophocles's question, 'Who is the slayer, who the victim? Speak.' And to answer, there are only people, everywhere, forming their multitudes, singly, so different and alike. The United Nations Assembly represents their hope organized; the atomic cataclysm the potentiality of obliteration, futility. At the end again are the children, playing: embodiments of a new world, as in W. Eugene Smith's classic photograph of a little boy and girl walking hand in hand through woods into sunlight.

This 'text' is given almost wholly in pictures alone.

The thematic epigrams are strophic guides, marking the stanzas. Such deliberate use of pictures is no longer novel; this is precisely the point to be noted. The achievement of 'The Family of Man' lies in its linguistic sophistication, rather than origination. Not long ago, the exhibition would have been generally abstruse—or even unintelligible—for most of the people who comprehend it immediately today. Its use of photographs, and of a museum's space to present them, follows and pre-requires an expanding familiarity with the terms and grammar of a complex pictorial language—itself one of the unique developments in communication of our century.

The first element of this language is photography, whose images of the world have become part of everyday vision in the past hundred years. But its visual syntax has developed only in a generation or two—looking back from the picture magazines, which revolutionized journalism in the 1930s; to the upheaval in spatial design that stirred a little more than sixty years ago, and produced a new painting, sculpture, architecture—and a new format for presenting words and pictures, the modern magazine page-spread; to that organic element that imparts more than unitary meanings to the pictures when they are grouped together: *montage,* that was learned from the motion picture.

'The Family of Man', in fact, is the most spectacular demonstration in recent years of the influence of the cinema in the visual arts. The photographs are not exhibited in the old, salon manner of the pictorialists, derived from ways of looking at paintings—each separately framed and contained, in form as well as content. They were selected and ordered to create a picture story— much as picture stories are synthesized in magazines and books. Each section, in its own room or part of the museum display, corresponds to a 'spread' in a picture magazine—and, especially, to a sequence in a film, with the vital filmic element of time suggested by a pictorial rhythm that is analogous to the rhythm created in editing a motion picture.

The eye leaps from one photograph to the next—not

haphazardly, but by design. The mind associates its images—not in any accidental pattern of fragments, but in a *gestalt* or configuration, or form-relationship, that was deliberately intended, and deliberately created by careful choice and discard, juxtaposition and emphatic isolation. If we had not learned, since we were children, to follow the montage or combination of separate shots in a movie, we would be unable to 'read' the picture story—in a museum display, or in magazines and newspapers, or even in comic strips, which are so filmic as to resemble the story boards or visual synopses used in the production of motion pictures.

The eye moves around the typical magazine story-spread according to the design in which the pictures have been arranged—and this layout is the practical application of principles that were developed during modern artists' exploration of relations in two- and three-dimensional space. We may regard the abstractions of the De Stijl movement—exemplified by van Doesburg, Huszár, and most famously, Piet Mondrian—as Western sophistications of the linear simplicities of Japanese graphic design and architecture. But they have had profound practical consequences—as in providing the formal idiom wherein to arrange the structural elements of steel and glass, in Lever House or the United Nations; or the discipline whereby the eye may travel over the precisely mapped routes of adverstising display—or, reading a magazine story, from pictures to text, or from pictures to pictures, in an exact, orderly manner. 'The Family of Man' exhibition was designed to reapply this discipline to three-dimensional space.

As Paul Rudolph has created the basic installation, the viewer is directed to walk and see in a way quite similar to that whereby the eye moves over a picture magazine or book. But the design of a picture story, whether on paper or on walls or partitions in a museum, serves only to provide direction for the appreciation of content. And the modern language of photographs, that has become one of the great tongues of the earth, depends upon a grammar which we had to master first in order to comprehend the movies. It is a language in whose terms we may formulate our knowledge of the world, and speak of it to others. It has orders of coherence, and requires a discipline for determining clarity and evaluating meaning. It does not simply reproduce reality, in an exact likeness, but recreates it according to a continually elaborating iconography.

The pioneer director, D. W. Griffith, who made *Birth of a Nation* and *Intolerance,* originating most of the essential elements of cinematic form, once remarked, 'The moving picture, although a growth of only a few years, is boundless in its scope and endless in its possibilities. . . . The task I'm trying to achieve is above all to make you see.' How much we have learned to see in the way of the cinema, albeit far from the theatres and their quickening screens, may be the deepest meaning of Steichen's 'The Family of Man.'